Your guide to the

# STRANGEST
# UNDERGROUND PLACES
# IN BRITAIN

*- and the best worldwide -*

*FRONT COVER PICTURES*

*top left - London Dungeon - page 14*
*top right - Hall of Bones - page 66*
*bottom left - Cheddar Caves - page 32*
*bottom right - Poole's Cavern - page 23*

# STRANGEST
## UNDERGROUND
## PLACES IN BRITAIN
### - and the best worldwide -

TITLE NUMBER 3. FIRST EDITION.

## WRITTEN & PUBLISHED BY
## STRANGEST BOOKS

*Published in England by Strangest Books (http://www.strangestbooks.co.uk).*
*Text, design and complete contents copyright, 2006, is the property of*
*Strangest Books in accordance with the Copyright, Designs and Patents Act 1988.*

*ACKNOWLEDGEMENTS*

*Thanks are given to those people who have kindly provided some of the photographs for inclusion*
*in this book. These photographs are reproduced with the permission of the relevant copyright holders.*
*Certain images appear from public domain.*

*This book is the result of extensive research and the entries contained herein are inserted at the sole*
*discretion of the publishers. This does not indicate a preference over establishments not included.*
*The publishers receive no payments or inducements for inclusion in this book.*

# foreword

Most of us can clearly remember a time when we saw or read about something that was so strange or unusual it made us gasp in wonder, or even sent a cold chill through our body.

The Strangest series of Books has the very best compilations of all that is weird, amazing and bizarre in Britain (and the rest of the world) today, and will open up a wonderland of curiosities for you to discover - most of which you probably never knew existed.

Each of the books in our series covers a chosen subject and will provide you with a thoroughly entertaining read. There are fascinating, mysterious, and very often unbelievable places and things to be seen. Some are so unusual that only a visit to actually see for yourself will suffice, or you can simply experience an unforgettable bedtime read, and then amaze your friends and colleagues with some of the startling facts.

Sure to provide readers with as much pleasure as they did for the researchers, the Strangest series of Books can be purchased or ordered from all good book stores and high street retailers. Information on how to order direct can be found on page 96.

*Except a living man, there is nothing more wonderful than a book.*

**- Charles Kingsley**

# about this book

When we think of the world beneath our feet visions of mysterious places, mystical caverns, and the devil himself springs to mind. The most unusual places you can visit below ground can be found in this book - Strangest Underground Places in Britain *and the best worldwide* - including a street of shops and houses sealed and entombed following the plague, massive power stations in hollow mountains, prehistoric burial grounds, and the secrets of mystery hill.

The Ming Tombs, prisons and dungeons, the amazing underground cathedral made of salt, the hall of bones, subterranean concerts, and even a complete town that is built almost entirely underground. Volcanic caves, crystal caves, and bizarre caves, or what about the experience of a lifetime at the fantastic glow-worm caves where millions of these tiny living lights can be seen.

Ghosts, demons, cosmic caverns, lost world caverns, treasure caves, they are all here in a book you will want to read more than once - Strangest Underground Places in Britain *and the best worldwide.*

# alphabetical index of entries

## Part One - BRITAIN

**BUCKINGHAMSHIRE**
Hellfire Caves, West Wycombe - haunted caves and a stolen heart - page 24

**CHESHIRE**
Hack Green Secret Nuclear Bunker, Nantwich - see the 'fallout' room - page 28

**CORNWALL**
Charlestown Shipwreck, Rescue & Heritage Centre, Helston - bits from boats - page 44
Poldark Mine, Helston - recreated tin mine - page 44
Carnglaze Slate Caverns, Liskeard - underground concerts held here - page 25
Geevor Tin Mine, Penzance - old tin mines that go under the Atlantic - page 27

**CUMBRIA**
Florence Mine, Egremont - last deep iron ore mine in Europe - page 33

**DERBYSHIRE**
Poole's Cavern, Buxton - the Filch of Bacon & Poached Egg Chamber - page 23
Blue John Cavern, Hope Valley - Blue John fluor-spar cavern - page 41
Peak Cavern, Hope Valley - largest cave entrance in UK at the Devil's Arse - page 41
Speedwell Cavern, Hope Valley - underground canal and the Bottomless Pit - page 41
Treak Cliff Cavern, Hope Valley - the miniature grottoes of Fairyland - page 41
Heights of Abraham, Matlock Bath - cable car journey to the underground - page 42

**DEVON**
Beer Quarry Caves, Seaton - bats and building blocks in Beer - page 34
Morwellham Quay, Tavistock - electric tramway trip into the mine - page 27
Kents Cavern, Torquay - first occupied 31,000 years ago - page 36

**ESSEX**
Kelvedon Hatch Bunker, Kelvedon Hatch - 75ft deep Cold War bunker - page 28
Essex Secret Bunker, Mistley - huge subterranean nuclear-ready complex - page 28

**GLOUCESTERSHIRE**
Clearwell Caves, Royal Forest of Dean - crystals, minerals and ochres - page 39

**HERTFORDSHIRE**
Royston Cave, Royston - mysterious medieval carvings - page 34
Scott's Grotto, Ware - folly which took 30 years to build - page 26
Welwyn Roman Baths, Welwyn - 1,700 year old Roman villa under the A1 (M) - page 46

## KENT
Chislehurst Caves, Chislehurst - 20 mile labyrinth of tunnels and caverns - page 39
Dover Castle Secret Wartime Tunnels, Dover - as the name says - page 44
Margate Shell Grotto, Margate - 2,000 year old shell temple - page 26

## LONDON
London Dungeon, SE1 - macabre dungeon with chilling tableaux - page 14
Winston Churchill's Britain at War Experience, SE1 - all about the war - page 40
Cabinet War Rooms, SW1A - and more about the war - page 40

## MERSEYSIDE
Western Approaches, Liverpool - over 100 gas-proof & bomb-proof rooms - page 43
Williamson's Tunnels, Liverpool - why are they here & what are they for? - page 43

## NOTTINGHAMSHIRE
Caves of Nottingham, Nottingham - old Nottingham depicted underground - page 21
Cresswell Crags, Worksop - Britain's only known Ice Age rock art - page 39

## SCOTLAND
Cruachan Power Station , Argyll - power station inside a mountain - page 16
Auld Reekie Tours, Edinburgh - most haunted, the plague & pagan temple - page 35
Edinburgh Dungeon, Edinburgh - notorious villains & gruesome surgery - page 14
Mercat Tours, Edinburgh - the supernatural and the ghastly underground - page 35
Scotland's Secret Bunker, Fife - 100ft underground and 15ft thick - page 28
Skara Brae, Orkney - Neolithic underground settlement - page 20

## SHROPSHIRE
Hawkstone Park and Follies, Shrewsbury - grottoes & secret tunnels - page 38
The Tar Tunnel, Telford - as the name would imply - page 17

## SOMERSET
Cheddar Caves & Gorge, Cheddar - earliest case of cannibalism in Britain - page 32
Wookey Hole, Wells - the Witch of Wookey - page 18

## SUSSEX
Smugglers Adventure, Hastings - supernatural manifestations & Hairy Jack - page 31

## WALES
King Arthur's Labyrinth, Mid Wales - mystery and legends - page 45
Electric Mountain, North Wales - subterranean power station - page 16
Gloddfa Ganol Slate Mine, North Wales - world's largest slate mine - page 25
Great Orme Mines, North Wales - Bronze Age copper mine - page 27
Llechwedd Slate Caverns, North Wales - ride the miners tramway - page 25
Sygun Copper Mine, North Wales - winding tunnels and huge chambers - page 27
Dan-yr-Ogof Showcaves, South Wales - largest showcaves in UK - page 19
Dolaucothi Gold Mines, West Wales - ancient gold mine - page 27

## WEST MIDLANDS
Holy Austin Rock Houses, Stourbridge - troglodyte dwellings - page 38

## YORKSHIRE
Ingleborough Cave, Clapham - network of sculpted passages - page 34
Stump Cross Caverns, Harrogate - wolverines were here - page 34
White Scar Cave, Ingleton - longest showcave in Britain - page 39
York Dungeon, York - torture, plague, and the pit of despair - page 14

# Part Two - USA

## ARKANSAS
Cosmic Cavern - unique cave formations and gemstone panning - page 59
Old Spanish Treasure Cave - is there $40 million worth of treasure here? - page 56

## CALIFORNIA
Forestiere Underground Gardens - amazing underground house and gardens - page 50

## CONNECTICUT
Old Newgate Prison & Copper Mine - old lags accommodation - page 49

## IOWA
Grotto of the Redemption - largest grotto in the world - page 48

## KENTUCKY
Mammoth Cave - longest cave in the world - page 61

## MINNESOTA
Niagara Cave - Paul Bunyan's Bed and the Wedding Chapel - page 52

## MISSOURI
Bridal Cave - wacky underground weddings - page 52
Brunson Instrument Company - 20,000sq metre underground factory - page 56
Fantastic Caverns - the blind Ozarks cavefish - page 54
Meramec Caverns - gunpowder, Jesse James, & underground bodybuilding - page 53
Underground Racquets Ltd - anyone for tennis, underground - page 53

## MONTANA
Radon Health Mine - subterranean radiation healing - page 56

## NEW HAMPSHIRE
Mystery Hill - America's underground Stonehenge - page 58

## NEW MEXICO
Kokopelli's Cave Bed & Breakfast - underground digs - page 49

## OHIO
Haunted Cave - Halloween horrors and 30,000 brown bats - page 56

## TENNESSEE
Crystal Shrine Grotto - strange underground shrine to Christ - page 60
The Lost Sea - possibly the largest underground body of water in the world - page 57

## TEXAS
Cascade Caverns - the Giant Molar and 100ft waterfall - page 62
Inner Space Caverns - the Flowing Stone of Time & the Lake of the Moon - page 64

## VIRGINIA
Luray Caverns - world's only stalacpipe organ - page 62
Shenandoah Caverns - the Grotto of the Gods - page 64

## WEST VIRGINIA
Lost World Caverns - 30 ton Snowy Chandelier and 'Bat Boy' - page 57

# Part Three - REST OF WORLD

**AUSTRALIA**
Argyle Diamond Mine - world's largest diamond producer - page 94
Coober Pedy - amazing underground town - page 85
Marakoopa Caves - cave rivers and huge caverns - page 86
Naracoorte Caves - batting on an infra-red wicket - page 86
Wellington Caves - the giant kangaroo & the Altar Rock - page 86

**AUSTRIA**
Hall of Bones-Beinhaus - sun bleached skulls and bones in a charnel house - page 66

**BELIZE**
Barton Creek Cave - the Underworld and place of virgin sacrifices - page 72

**BERMUDA**
Crystal Caves of Bermuda - splendid subterranean discovery - page 94

**CANADA**
Diefenbunker - Canada's Cold War complex - page 90
Montreal Underground City - largest underground complex in the world - page 85

**CHINA**
Beijing Underground City - underground business & shopping, Chinese style - page 85
Dragon Palace - the wonderland of the Dragon King - page 68
Ming Tombs - the mausoleums of 13 emperors - page 88
Yungang Grottoes - 51,000 stone carvings in 52 caves - page 71

**FRANCE**
The Catacombs of Paris - the Empire of Death - page 78

**GERMANY**
Nuremberg Art Bunker - art treasures depository during the war - page 73

**INDIA**
Elephanta Caves - magnificent cave temple and shrine to Shiva - page 68

**ISRAEL**
Grotto of Gethsemane - religious cave in the Holy Land - page 82
Grotto of the Nativity - place of Jesus' birth - page 82
Milk Grotto Chapel - the place to be for mums to be - page 82

**ITALY**
Capuchin Catacombs - the Museum of Death - page 76
Christian Catacombs of Rome - hundreds of miles of the dead - page 78
Fontanelle Cemetery - millions of bones piled high - page 66
Villa Torlonia-Mussolini's Bunker - network of Jewish catacombs - page 90

**JAPAN**
Akiyoshi-do Cave - largest calcareous cave in the land of the rising sun - page 71

## KOREA
3rd Infiltration Tunnel  - one way to invade your neighbours - page 93

## MALAYSIA
Batu Caves - a million devotees get hooked here - page 75
Deer Cave - Abraham Lincoln's double in bat land - page 72

## MALDIVES
Ithaa Undersea Restaurant - eating with the fishes - page 69

## NEW ZEALAND
Waitomo Glow-Worm Caves - a galaxy of millions of tiny lights - page 81

## POLAND
Sztolnie Kowary  - old uranium production site - page 94
Wieliczka Salt Mine - underground cathedral carved from salt - page 91
Wolf's Lair - Hitler's fortress of bunkers - page 83

## SPAIN
Jameos del Agua - concert hall, bars and restaurant in caves - page 72

## SWITZERLAND
Fortress Furigen - enter a world of Swiss secrecy - page 90

## TURKEY
Cave Church - Grotto of St.Peter in Antioch - first church built by man - page 82
Underground Cities of Cappadocia - 1200BC subterranean towns & cities - page 85

## VIETNAM
Cu Chi Tunnels - 75 mile relic of the Vietnam War - page 89

# Part One
## - BRITAIN -

*Now in use for concerts and other events, the old Rum Store at Carnglaze Caverns has superb acoustics and can seat up to 400 people - page 25.*

# - daunting dungeons -

## THE DUNGEONS
comprising:

## LONDON DUNGEON
**Tooley Street, London SE1**
**Tel: 0207 403 7221**

## YORK DUNGEON
**12 Clifford Street, York,**
**Yorkshire. Tel: 01904 632599**

## EDINBURGH DUNGEON
**31 Market Street, Edinburgh,**
**Scotland. Tel: 0131 240 1001**

The Dungeons are some of Europe's premier themed attractions offering visitors the opportunity to take a terrifying journey through the darker side of history. At present there are 5 Dungeon attractions; London, York and Edinburgh as listed above, and others in Hamburg and Amsterdam. Each attraction depicts history and events relevant to their own region in a quite chilling yet entertaining way. Often gory but always realistic tableaux, accompanied by haunting sound effects, depict everything from the notorious serial killer Jack the Ripper to a vivid recreation of the plague at the disease-ridden city of York in the 14th century.

The following is only a brief summary of what each Dungeon has to offer as re-investment programmes and frequent new tableaux and exhibits ensure the Dungeons remain Europe's most thrilling and chilling attractions.

London Dungeon is Europe's largest 'dark' visitor attraction and is appropriately sited under the bleak, foreboding arches of London Bridge. It is certainly not for the faint-hearted and visitors see torture, execution, and macabre medieval madness along the way. The Great Fire of London, a Boat Ride to Hell, and the Labyrinth of the Lost are all fantastic multi-million pound themed attractions amongst dozens of other exhibits and tableaux. Live actors add to the terror and excitement. There are many hideous instruments of torture

*Horrific torture depicted at the York Dungeon.*

*The London Dungeon.*
*What a way to go.*

*A novel welcome to the*
*Edinburgh Dungeon.*

to be seen in recreated settings, most of which are unbelievably sadistic and cruel.

The dangerous streets of Whitechapel in Victorian London were the hunting grounds for notorious murderer and mutilator Jack the Ripper. One of the most infamous serial killers of all time, you can meet Jack at the London Dungeon. The venue is also available for exclusive evening hire for a party with a 'cutting-edge'.

Live costumed 'characters' are an integral part of the Dungeon experience and at York Dungeon they are quite striking. 'Plague' is a vivid recreation of what 14th century York was like when infected rats spread the Black Death. The Pit of Despair, Witch Trials, Gorvik - the real Viking story, and the lost phantom Roman Legion are all first class attractions. No visit to York would be complete without meeting some of the historical figures who have links to the

city and here you have the chance to meet Guy Fawkes, notorious for the Gunpowder Plot, and the most famous highwayman of them all - Dick Turpin.

Many of our ancestors most vile means of inflicting excruciating pain on their prisoners can be seen at Edinburgh Dungeon such as thumb-screws, flesh tearers and muscle clamps. Scotland, particularly Edinburgh, has had a fair share of horrific events, notorious characters, and general misery over the centuries. Early surgery in all its gruesome aspects can be witnessed here, you can enter the cave of one of the country's most notorious villains - Sawney Bean, hear the story of Burke and Hare who were murderers who sold their victims for surgical training, and see torture, disease, and evil deeds all around you. Screaming prisoners, spitting demons, and a whole lot more awaits you at the Edinburgh Dungeon.

## CRUACHAN POWER STATION
**Cruachan Visitor Centre,
Dalmally, Argyll, Scotland
Tel: 01866 822618**

Visitors to Cruachan Power Station travel 1km underground, deep within Ben Cruachan - the 'hollow mountain' - to see one of the most amazing engineering achievements the country has ever produced. This is the world's first high-head reversible, pumped storage hydro scheme and it is housed in a massive cavern within the mountain. There is little visible outward sign to indicate its presence here but for the new visitor's centre on the banks of Loch Awe, which is the starting point for guided tours.

Your visit to the underground generation hall takes you past tropical plants which thrive under unique conditions. Here, in this cavernous chamber, 4 x 134,000 horsepower reversible pump-turbines each drive powerful motor-generators which takes water up to a reservoir at off-peak, and top up the grid at other times of the day. They can produce enough electricity to supply a city the size of Edinburgh, or can pump an incredible 120 tons of water per second.

This was certainly an enormous feat of civil engineering in building the dam, and excavating the machinery hall and thousands of metres of tunnels. From the exhibition centre, where you learn about electricity and its production at Cruachan, an electric mini-bus takes you into the legendary Ben Cruachan itself and the visitors gallery of the echoey 91 metres x 36 metres underground generation hall. You are now 365 metres below the Cruachan Reservoir. Amazing stuff!

## ELECTRIC MOUNTAIN
**Llanberis, Gwynedd,
North Wales. Tel: 01286 870636**

Towering mountains and the splendid scenery of Snowdonia greet visitors to Electric Mountain, First Hydro Company's visitor centre in Llanberis and your starting point for a tour of Dinorwig Power Station. From the visitor centre a First Hydro bus transports you to the power station itself, descending deep inside the ancient Elidir Mountain's labyrinth of dark, and somewhat spooky tunnels.

This, again, is one of the world's marvels of engineering and construction. Dinorwig provides instant 'on-demand' power and is reputed to have the fastest response of any power station in the world. It is capable of providing 1,800 megawatts of electricity from standby in just 10 seconds. Using pumped storage, Dinorwig uses the kinetic energy of water flowing from an upper reservoir to produce electricity by way of turbo-generators. They can also work in reverse to pump water back into the high level reservoir at night, using excess power from the national grid when electricity costs are low. Sounds somewhat like an enormous battery.

Your bus transportation takes you half a mile into the mountain to the machinery hall. Upon arrival, the sheer scale of the station is quite a shock. The sound of machinery is everywhere. A gigantic cavern was blasted out of the heart of the mountain to accommodate all the machinery and equipment and the area you stand within is said to be about the size of 2 giant cathedrals. Most of the operations here are controlled automatically and in many instances only a single operative oversees the controls from high up in the control room.

## THE TAR TUNNEL
### Adjacent to Coalport China Museum, Coalport, Telford, Shropshire. Tel: 01952 884391

Discovered over 200 years ago The Tar Tunnel was dug from the hillside in 1787, most likely in connection with local coal workings. The workers struck an underground spring that gushed forth a thick viscous substance - subsequently identified as bitumen - which was thereafter used to treat ropes, and also implemented as waterproofing (caulking) for ships.

*Bitumen still seeps from the walls more than 200 years after it was first discovered.*

*Peering into the gloom of the Tar Tunnel.*

It was quite an amazing sight to see this natural phenomenon in the 18th century and many other uses were soon found for the newly discovered bitumen. Remarkably, it was also processed and bottled before being sold as 'Betton's British Oil', as a remedy for rheumatic problems, albeit only in small amounts.

*Bitumen (also called asphalt or tar) is the dark brown or black viscous residue remaining from the vacuum distillation of crude petroleum. It also occurs in nature and some geologists believe that naturally occurring deposits of bitumen would have been formed from the remains of ancient microscopic algae and other such things that lived long ago. One source has stated that "it is possible that bitumens are primordial material formed during accretion of the earth and reworked by bacteria that consume hydrocarbons". Bitumens are also found in meteorites, copper, and caves.*

*Most bitumens contain sulphur, lead, mercury, and even arsenic. Other toxic elements are also common. Asphalt, commonly used for road surfacing, is a mixture of mineral aggregate and bitumen and is often referred to as tarmac. The word 'tar' refers to the black viscous material that results from the destructive distillation of coal.*

*Serene and enchanting; a shallow pool and colourful reflections in the caverns of Wookey Hole and (below), is this the face of the Witch of Wookey which can be seen at the caves today?*

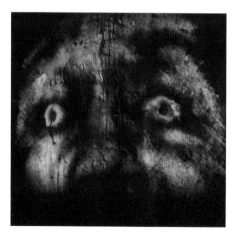

## WOOKEY HOLE
**Wookey Hole, Wells, Somerset. Tel: 01749 672243**

Powerful forces formed the spectacular caves of Wookey Hole. Chamber 3 (known as the Witch's Parlour) was carved out by an underground river over a million years ago, and it was the Legend of the Witch of Wookey that many say made King Arthur come over from Avalon to slay her. Others say that an abbot exorcised her and turned her to stone by sprinkling holy water on her. Legend says that she was an old woman who lived alone in the caves, except for her dog and some goats, but folklore is an abstruse subject and time frequently obscures its origins. What is known as factual about Wookey Hole is that it was a habitat of the Celts - with Chamber 4 in use as a burial chamber - and that man has lived in and around the caves for over 50,000 years. In fact the caves are millions of years old and contain many mysteries.

Ancient bones of animals such as mammoth, lion and bear have been found here, and today the caves have freshwater shrimps, a variety of insects, and horseshoe bats which hibernate here. The subterranean River Axe can be seen flowing into Wookey Gorge, the Caves Museum tells the story of 50,000 years habitation of the caves, and there is plenty of entertainment whatever the weather for all the family. The caverns are as high as cathedrals, the Hyena Den has 70,000 year old camp fires, and the landscape and scenery are superb. What are you waiting for?

## DAN-YR-OGOF SHOWCAVES

**near Abercraf,**
**Upper Swansea Valley,**
**South Wales. Tel: 01639 730284**

Dan-yr-Ogof literally means 'below the cave' and apart from being one of the largest showcaves in the UK it is the largest cave complex in Western Europe. They were discovered in 1912 by 2 brothers (Jeff and Ashwell Morgan) from Tymawr who found 3 lakes, a waterfall, and quite magnificent chambers. In 1937 more experienced cavers from Yorkshire explored the caves, and in 1953 the Cathedral Cave was explored and the Dome of St Paul's where a lake is fed by cascading waterfalls.

In the main showcave visitors walk for half a mile seeing spectacular stalactite and stalagmite formations, whilst the Cathedral Cave is named after its main feature - a huge chamber, the 42ft high 'Dome of St Paul's'. The Bone Cave is so called as about 50 human skeletons have been found there, many dating back over 3,000 years to the Bronze Age. Here there are displays about an early cave settlement and archaeology. In fact Dan-yr-Ogof has been classed as a 'Site of Special Scientific Interest' and, based on archaeological evidence uncovered, the life-size replicas you will see give a realistic look at how people must have lived during the Bronze Age.

Families are well catered for at this first-class attraction. The extensive site has Northern Europe's largest award-winning Dinosaur Park, a Shire Horse Centre, a replica Iron Age Farm, and a wide range of other family orientated

activities and attractions. Dan-yr-Ogof Showcaves are only 20 minutes from the M4 Motorway, half-way between Brecon and Swansea.

## SKARA BRAE
**Orkney, Scotland**
**Tel: 0845 225 5121**

This is possibly Orkney's most visited site and is regarded as one of the most important monuments in Europe. Orkney has long been associated with bad weather and fierce storms due to its location, but the winter of 1850 saw a great storm that, coupled with devastating winds and very high tides, stripped grass and sand from a large mound. This revealed the outline of stone buildings, and the local laird (William Watt of Skail) began an excavation of the site. The remains of 4 ancient houses were unearthed and although the site was then left undisturbed, another bad storm in 1925 prompted further digging. More dwellings were discovered over the years which at first were believed to be part of an ancient Iron Age settlement, but subsequent radio-carbon dating showed they dated from the late Neolithic period and would have been inhabited between 3200BC and 2200BC. It is now known that over 4,000 years ago a massive sandstorm engulfed the village of Skara Brae causing the people to flee and leave behind their belongings. Excavations have discovered these belongings, furnishings, and stone dwellings completely intact due to the preotection of the sand that cocooned the settlement for over 4,000 years.

Each house shares an identical design and a network of narrow stone passages linked them together. At just over a metre high, the passages had stone slab roofs and were covered over with insulating 'midden'. One main passageway led into the village and at either side of the entrance was a bar-hole that indicated it could have been sealed against intruders.

Visitors to the village today would think this is the remains of an underground village but that is not strictly true. The houses were not sunk into the ground but were actually built into mounds of waste and rubbish known as 'midden'. During its lifetime the village became embedded in this rubbish and merged together, and to this extent (appearing as just a low flat mound from a distance) it could be said to be underground.

Because of the notorious Orkney weather that is the cause of so much erosion, Skara Brae now stands by the shore. The village of over 40 centuries ago would have been a good distance from the sea.

*The earliest houses in the village were circular with one main room that would have contained the central hearth, either side of which were beds set into the walls. There would have been a shelved stone dresser, and the door to the house would have been a large slab of stone that could be held in place by a bar slotted into 'bar-holes', to prevent entry. Life inside the houses, or huts, would have been reasonably comfortable due to the overlying midden insulation. Beds would usually have had straw mattresses and sheepskin or deerskin coverings. Because of the covered stone passages it would have been possible to go from house to house without venturing out into a dreadful Orkney winter. Later houses in the village followed the same design but on a larger scale, although the beds were no longer built into the walls but projected out.*

## CAVES OF NOTTINGHAM
**Drury Walk, Upper Level,
Broad Marsh Shopping Centre,
Nottingham, Nottinghamshire
Tel: 0115 924 1424**

The Soft Sherwood Sandstone beneath the city centre of Nottingham permitted the easy digging out of many cellars and caves, and over the past 800 years or so over 400 caves were cut out and utilised for a variety of uses such as air-raid shelters, storerooms, and even dwellings. Many have been destroyed due to development but the Caves of Nottingham, unusually located beneath a modern shopping centre, was saved thanks to voluntary groups. Opened in 1994 as an attraction, its main feature is the Pillar Cave & Tannery. This is probably the oldest of the caves which dates back to 1250 and it features the remains of Britain's only medieval underground tannery. It is called the Pillar Cave because of the striking central pillar within.

Drury Hill was one of the oldest streets in Nottingham until it was demolished in 1968. One area of the cave shows what this narrow cobbled street looked like. Many of the caves were used as slum dwellings and the Victorian Slum depicts the appalling conditions that had to be endured. The caves most recent use was as air-raid shelters during World War Two and the underground exhibition on this theme contains an array of wartime memorabilia.

*The Caves of Nottingham, located underneath Broadmarsh Shopping Centre, has Britain's only medieval underground tannery and a host of other interesting subterranean attractions.*

*Poole's Cavern - boasting some of the finest underground views in the country.*

# - poached egg chamber -

## POOLE'S CAVERN
**Green Lane, Buxton,
Derbyshire. Tel: 01298 26978**

Poole's Cavern has long been an exciting place to visit although it was not until 1854 that the cave's owner, the 6th Duke of Devonshire, had it transformed into a showcave for tourists. Mr Frank Redfern was the first appointed custodian and his first job was to make the cave more accessible. Blasting work was done to increase the height of the ceilings, 17 gas lamps were installed, and glacial sediment was removed. In 1976 the new owners - Buxton & District Civic Association - installed 100 electric lights, and today, visitors flock here to see what has been described as one of the finest underground views in the country. New caves have since been discovered at the end of the original showcave, and some of the beautiful formations that can now be seen are unrivalled anywhere.

It is possible that the cave has seen previous use as a Romano-British bronze jewellery workshop. Over a dozen items of Roman bronze jewellery were found during a dig in 1981, and during the 3 years following that over 4,000 items were unearthed including Roman Samian ware, pottery, Roman coins, leather, and animal bones. A selection of the items can be viewed at the visitor centre which also tells of the history of man's use of the cave over the past 5,000 years.

Sights to see at Poole's Cavern include the Roman Chamber (and archaeological dig), the Great Dome, Mary Queen of Scots Pillar, and the Flitch of Bacon Stalactite - so called because early visitors, in candlelight, thought it resembled a half a pig hanging in a butcher's shop. At well over 6ft it is the largest stalactite in Derbyshire and

would have been 3ft longer, had Victorian vandals not broke off the tip section of it.

The Poached Egg Chamber is said to be the highlight of the cavern. It is so called because of the orange tops on the 'poached egg' stalagmites. This results from a combination of iron-oxide in the rock above, and bacterial elements. Almost every possible type of cave formation can be seen in the Poached Egg Chamber, with some quite unique in the caving world.

Looking down from the bridge in the main showcave you can see 160 metres down the main river passage to the Roman Chamber. This is said to be the longest internal view in any British showcave.

# HELLFIRE CAVES
**West Wycombe,
Buckinghamshire
Tel: 01494 533739**

These caves were originally excavated during the 1750's and they are located on the site of an ancient quarry. There is a quite fascinating history connected with the caves that were said to be used for all sorts of mischief in bygone days.

They were excavated and fashioned by Sir Francis Dashwood (later to become Lord le Despencer) to provide work for unemployed farm workers following harvest failures. Dashwood was a notorious and extravagant Georgian prankster, often described as a rake, who took great pleasure in his many indulgences. Highly intelligent and a lover of the arts, he was also to see 20 years service as a Member of Parliament, become Chancellor of the Exchequer, and finally Postmaster General.

Dashwood also owned many clubs including the cheekily named Divan Club and the Lincoln. His grand tour of Europe and the Ottoman Empire was instrumental in not only the naming of his clubs, but also the inspiration for the design of Hellfire Caves. He was a leading member of the Dilettanti Society and also a secret society called 'The Knights of St.Francis of Wycombe', which later came to be called the Hell-Fire Club.

From the 1740's until about 1763 the Hell-Fire Club met at Medmenham Abbey on the River Thames. Members here, in the guise of monks, were said to indulge in sexual frolics in the company of assorted women (or 'nuns' as they would be referred to). It appears that the club was little more than an excuse for wild drinking, profane revels, and a general good time. Reputedly, this burned down accidentally, and subsequent meetings were held in the caves. These meetings were some 300ft below ground and approximately half a mile from the entrance.

As was fashionable at the time the caves are meant to represent many things. The Inner Temple, Catacombs of Rome, and The Triangle whose shape is said to be part of a woman's anatomy are all prime examples. The splendid Banqueting Hall is an enormous cavern and considering it was dug by hand is quite remarkable. You can almost sense the grand parties that must have been held here. It is in fact available for private hire today. Originally a boat ride would have been the only means of reaching the Inner Temple within the caves complex, but a bridge has now been built for the use of visitors.

There are many strange tales connected with the caves. According to legend the River Styx separates our world from the underworld, and ghostly tales abound concerning hauntings. Sir Paul Whitehead was a former steward of the Hell-Fire Club and was devoted to the 'Knights of St.Francis'. His last will and testament requested that upon his death an urn be placed in the Dashwood Museum (directly above the caves) containing his heart, as he wished it to remain with the Dashwood's forever. This may have happened but in 1829 it is said to have been stolen by an Australian soldier, and Whitehead's ghost is now said to haunt the caves.

It may never be known what prompted a man of Dashwood's standing to excavate the caves, or indulge in such behaviour, after all here is a man who would become a future peer of the realm. The answer is still a riddle but the Georgian grotto and tunnels within the caves remain.

# - underground concerts on the slate -

## CARNGLAZE SLATE CAVERNS
**St.Neot, Liskeard, Cornwall**
**Tel: 01579 320251**

Carnglaze is located in the valley of the River Loveny, a tributary of the Fowey. In Cornish, Carnglaze means 'blue-green rock pile', and the mud that would become the slate that is now Carnglaze was laid down underneath the seas as long ago as 500 million years.

There are 3 caverns that comprise Carnglaze including the amazing Cathedral Cavern, and the famous subterranean lake must be seen with its crystal clear blue-green water. The Rum Store Cavern is quite unique. It was used by the Royal Navy during the Second World War to store their supplies of rum - hence the name. Over 90 metres long and 20 metres wide, in 2001 it was converted into an auditorium with seating for 400. The acoustics are outstanding and have been acclaimed by many international performers who have played here. Underground concerts, how unusual.

## LLECHWEDD SLATE CAVERNS
**Blaenau Ffestiniog, Gwynedd,**
**North Wales. Tel: 01766 830306**

Slate, probably the most famous product of Snowdonia, is extracted at a number of sites in this area, and Llechwedd Slate Caverns are probably the most spectacular. The Miners Underground Tramway, opened in 1972, takes you through enormous caverns of cathedral proportions. An ingeniously designed vehicle takes passengers down a 30 degree incline into the depths of the mine.

## GLODDFA GANOL SLATE MINE
**Blaenan Ffestiniog, Gwynedd,**
**North Wales. Tel: 01766 830664**

At the world's largest slate mine visitors can see open-cast blasting, restored miners cottages, and much more.

*A most unique experience; underground concerts are held at 'The Rum Store', part of an underground complex at Carnglaze Slate Caverns. Boasting breathtaking acoustics, this previously saw use as a rum store for the Royal Navy.*

## SCOTT'S GROTTO
**Scotts Road, Ware,
Hertfordshire
Tel: 01920 464131**

Scott's Grotto was built for John Scott, an 18th century poet and devout Quaker who was born in Bermondsey in 1730. He moved to Hertfordshire in 1740 to benefit from the cleaner air and inherited Amwell House in 1768 when his father died. Building grottoes was quite fashionable at this time so Scott decided to have one of his own, and what a grotto it is. It is said to have cost in excess of £10,000 to construct and taken 30 years to complete.

Scott's Grotto is a series of interconnected chambers and tunnels which are lined with shells, coloured pieces of glass and knapped flints. The chambers extend some 67ft into the chalk hillside and would have been a huge undertaking to construct. There are chambers with inexplicable names here such as the Committee Room, the Consultation Room, and the Robing Room, each a splendid achievement in shell and flint work. Scott's fairy-tale grotto is a superb example of excess and eccentricity of a past age.

## MARGATE SHELL GROTTO
**Grotto Hill, Margate, Kent
Tel: 01843 220008**

The origins of this grotto are unclear. It is probably the only underground shell temple in the world and is undoubtedly man-made, but was only accidentally discovered in 1835, with the first paying visitors descending the chalk steps in 1837. Millions of shells (over 50 different types) have been used to decorate over 2,000sq.ft of snaking passageways and most have exquisite mosaic designs. Even the roof is covered in complex shell patterns and the grotto is believed to be over 2,000 years old, although some designs of Egypt and India here would suggest it is much younger. Dating it is difficult as the shells are covered in soot from the gas lamps used to light the grotto in Victorian times. Carbon dating has been tried but the results were inconclusive.

The grotto is entered down a flight of steps which lead into a curved passage. This in turn leads into the Rotunda (a circular chamber), and a further passage leads off into the Dome with arches opening out in several directions. One of these arches leads to the Serpentine Passage which has some of the most striking mosaics and emblems here. Gods and goddesses, trees of life, and even phallic representations are all found at the Margate Shell Grotto, each a unique work of art.

It may never be known for certain what the grotto represents or when exactly it was made, but the excavation of it and the transporting and sorting of about 5 million shells would have been a mammoth task.

# - gold, copper and tin -

## DOLAUCOTHI GOLD MINES
**Pumpsaint, Llanwrda, Carmarthenshire, West Wales. Tel: 01558 650177**

There's gold in them thar hills. There certainly is at Dolaucothi Gold Mines which is said to be the only location in Britain where the Romans mined for the golden stuff. There is a wealth of surface and underground activities here including the chance to try your hand at gold-panning. Great fun.

## GREAT ORME MINES
**Great Orme, Llandudno, North Wales. Tel: 01492 870447**

This unique and exceptionally important site is the only Bronze Age copper mine in Europe that can be visited by the public. Explore the 3,500 year old passages, peer down a 470ft deep shaft, visit the Great Opencast, or see how our prehistoric ancestors turned rock into metal at the Smelting Site.

## SYGUN COPPER MINE
**Beddgelert, Gwynedd, North Wales. Tel: 01766 510101**

Copper was one of the first metals used by man and is part of the industrial heritage of North Wales. Sygun Copper Mine offers a rare opportunity of adventure and discovery in a mine that was abandoned in 1903. Winding tunnels, huge chambers, and copper ore veins which contain traces of gold, silver, and other precious metals can all be seen.

## GEEVOR TIN MINE
**Pendeen , Penzance, Cornwall Tel: 01736 788662**

Geevor Tin Mine is perched high on the rugged cliffs of Penwith overlooking the waves of the Atlantic on the western tip of Cornwall. It was founded in 1911 and provided work for countless thousands of men who laboured long hours in harsh conditions, with only a flickering candle to work by. The tunneling stretched out far into the Atlantic Ocean but the mine finally closed in 1990. Bought by Cornwall County Council in 1991, the site is now managed by Pendeen Community Heritage and offers a fascinating underground tour of this deep mine.

## MORWELLHAM QUAY
**Morwellham, near Tavistock, Devon. Tel: 01822 833808**

Morwellham Quay is the highest navigable point on the River Tamar and served as a port for the local communities over 1,000 years ago. First settled from about 970AD, Morwellham became famous for copper and at one time Morwellham Quay was hailed as 'the greatest port in Queen Victoria's empire'. By 1970 after centuries of activity everything closed, but the Morwellham and Tamar Trust was formed and conservation coupled with restoration means the area is once again thriving, albeit in a tourist attraction capacity. Visitors can now ride underground by electric train tramway into a copper mine that was last worked in 1869 and see marvellous displays of mining techniques throughout history.

## HACK GREEN SECRET NUCLEAR BUNKER
**French Lane End, Hack Green, Nantwich, Cheshire**
**Tel: 01270 629219**

This former World War 2 radar station and Government Headquarters building is now a Cold War museum and is an exciting day out for all the family, discovering the secret world of nuclear government. This astonishing concrete labyrinth was built in the 1960's when there was a real fear of a nuclear holocaust. It was where approximately 130 military commanders and civil servants would have been secreted away underground and ruled north-west England.

Visitors here get to experience a real 4 minute warning in addition to seeing tons of authentic equipment in their original settings. Offices, dormitories, canteen, scientists 'fallout' room, BBC studio, Minister of States office, sick bay, and a whole lot more will keep you entertained for hours. Several uncut broadcasts which were prepared for television airing, but never shown, can be seen, and children will love looking for the 'spy mice' hidden throughout the bunker.

## KELVEDON HATCH BUNKER
**Kelvedon Hatch, Essex**
**Tel: 01277 364883**

An amazing place, Kelvedon Hatch secret nuclear Bunker can be found by entering a nondescript bungalow in the middle of the Essex countryside. It is surrounded by farmland, and behind the blast screens that protect the bungalow

is the entrance to this 75ft deep underground bunker. It contains a maze of rooms, and reinforced concrete that is 10ft thick protects the complex. This old R4 Rotor bunker will spill all its secrets when you visit.

## ESSEX SECRET BUNKER
**Crown Buildings, Shrublands Road, Mistley, Essex**
**Tel: 01206 392271**

Packed with over 80 tons of authentic Cold War equipment, Essex Secret Bunker can be seen exactly as it would have been when prepared for nuclear armageddon. There are 3 cinemas that show Home Office civil defence training films, a 2-level operations centre, central map area, plant rooms, dormitory, offices, and much more to see and do at this 14,000 sq.ft complex. The once secret rooms reveal all their secrets, and sound effects and displays perfectly illustrate the story of what might have happened would this have become the 'hub' of Essex during a nuclear attack.

## SCOTLAND'S SECRET BUNKER
**Underground Nuclear Command Centre, Crown Buildings, St.Andrews, Fife, Scotland. Tel: 01333 310301**

This is another of the underground nuclear war command centres that was equipped in the early 1960's and is one of the most impressive. This amazing labyrinth was built 100ft underground; not that you would know from the innocent looking farmhouse that conceals the entrance. Encased in 15ft of reinforced concrete this is where military commanders and government officials would have controlled the country in the event that the UK were attacked, and a nuclear war started.

The design of the bunker required a 40 metre deep hole with a 'shock-absorbing' foundation of gravel. The outer shell of the structure with its huge, thick concrete casing was reinforced every 15cm with 2.5cm thick tungsten rods, and finally the complete structure was lined with brick, covered with netting, and soaked to form an outer casing. Although the guardhouse was built to resemble a traditional Scottish farmhouse it was secretly reinforced with concrete and steel girders. Finally, discrete landscaping gave no indication of the vast structure below.

A visit to this 24,000 sq.ft wonder starts by walking down the 150 metre entrance tunnel and through the massive hermetically sealed, 3 ton blast proof doors. You have now entered a world that would have been impossible to see for over 40 years as you start to explore the 2 underground levels of this immense place. The bunker contains an Operations Room, 2 cinemas, cafe, Royal Observer Corps Centre, the Minister of State's office, Plant Room, and numerous other offices and rooms. The offices of the emergency services, Met Office, scientific advisors and computer staff would surround the main command floor, and giant maps and charts would be used for up to the minute status information.

Staff in the bunker would have slept in one of the 6 dormitories which were capable of sleeping up to 300 personnel. They would sleep for 6 hours and then swap their bunks with another member of staff for the next 6 hours - a policy known as 'hot beds'. Hygiene would always be a problem as personnel would not have the luxury of a shower. Uncontaminated water would have been classed as a precious commodity so they may have had to go as long as 3 months underground without a shower or bath.

The Plant Room is quite amazing. The equipment here filters the air against radioactive particles and moves 1,500 cubic metres of air every minute. This in turn changes the entire air contents of the bunker every 15 minutes. Air can be ozonated or deozonated, humidified and dehumidified, and refrigerated or heated. In the event of a fire the smoke system can remove 2,200 cubic metres a minute, and should a power failure occur the bunker has its own emergency generator that can provide enough energy to supply a small city for weeks on end. A tour of the highly recommended Scotland's Secret Bunker will reveal many more startling facts.

*Knowing where you stand - nuclear wise - at Hack Green Secret Nuclear Bunker.*

BIKINI SECURITY STATES

The M.O.D has a series of coded colours which indicate the establishments state of alert.

WHITE – Situation stable
BLACK – Security is not guaranteed (Potential unrest)
SPECIAL BLACK – Terrorist threat exists
AMBER – High alert
RED – Full alert - The U.K. is at war with the possibility of nuclear attack

STATE OF SECURITY SPECIAL

## SMUGGLERS ADVENTURE
**St Clements Caves, West Hill, Hastings, Sussex**
**Tel: 01424 422964**

St Clements caves, on the slopes of West Hill in Hastings, is a cave system covering some 4 acres. They have a somewhat chequered history and are named after the nearby parish church. The first written reference to the caves is in 1786 when an old couple lived in them, although it is believed that they were in previous use as a hermitage for religious sects. They were largely forgotten until 1825 when Joseph Golding was smashing rock to create a seat in a West Hill Garden, and broke through to the caves. He modified and developed the caves extensively, opening them to the public in July 1827. Over 11 years of further excavation resulted in the 'Monks Walk' (seen opposite page), a 44 metre long dark passageway with 23 pillared niches for candles.

During the past 2 centuries the caves have seen a multitude of uses including being used as a military hospital for Wellington's troops, a smugglers contraband hideout, a World War Two air raid shelter, and a dancehall complete with waxworks exhibition.

Although having undergone many changes over the years it is the smuggling connections that stimulate most interest from the public. Now known as Smugglers Adventure, St Clements Caves has been transformed into a first class multi-media journey into the world of smuggling. The story of the Hastings smugglers is told by 'Hairy Jack', who also pops up in other places throughout your visit to tell you more about the smuggling deeds of himself and his friends. You will find out what happened when they got caught and what the punishment was. A fascinating sound and light show tells of the previous use of the caves as a tourist attraction.

Barely lit rock carved passageways and gloomy caves are home to dozens of life-sized figures that spring a few surprises; all accompanied by dramatic lighting and sound effects. There are also many old carvings in the caves and plenty visitors have reported unusual experiences, or remarked about the eerie atmosphere. The caves are in fact said to be haunted and an area known as 'The Chapel' has been the site of supernatural experiences and manifestations. Perhaps its an old sea-dog who wants his contraband back. An exciting hands-on adventure that is sure to be appreciated.

*The dangerous act of smuggling (above) and (opposite page) atmospheric and claustrophobic Monks Walk, both to be seen at St.Clements Caves.*

## CHEDDAR CAVES & GORGE
### Cheddar, Somerset
### Tel: 01934 742243

Cheddar Gorge has often been described as one of the wonders of England and this steep-sided canyon was carved out of the limestone during the Ice Age by an ancestor of the present Cheddar Yeo River. Here, the visitor will find the stunning Cheddar Caves, a wonderland for all age groups to explore.

Gough's Cave, the second of the 2 Cheddar Caves to be opened to the public, has a quite gruesome history. This is where the earliest authenticated case of cannibalism in Britain was discovered and the 5 skeletons (3 adults and 2 children) were scalped, de-fleshed, and eaten inside the cave 12,500 years ago. An exhibition on the subject of cannibalism at the caves provides much more information. Also discovered in Gough's Cave was 'Cheddar Man', a Mesolithic hunter-gatherer from 9,000 years ago. His bones comprise the oldest complete skeleton discovered in Britain and, quite remarkably, DNA tests have established a direct genetic link between him and a local schoolteacher - despite a gap of hundreds of generations.

Gough's Cave was discovered by a retired sea captain, Richard Cox Gough, who was the nephew of the then owner of the other Cheddar Cave now open to the public - Cox's Cave. Numerous flint and bone tools have been found at Gough's Cave but nothing surpasses the amazing flowstone sculptures of the Diamond Chamber, some of which have been well over 500,000 years in forming. Both Gough's Cave and Cox's Cave are without doubt some of the most beautifully decorated caves in Britain. Their Victorian discoverers installed mirror pools of water to reflect the stunning scenes and enhance the beauty of the delicate colours of the many stalagmites and stalactites.

Part of Cox's Cave is akin to a scene from a fantasy adventure. The Crystal Quest underground attraction consists of dragons, fairies and goblins, with a sprinkling of magic as good fights against evil. Children will really appreciate this delightful attraction but it is wise not to mention the strange phenomenon that surrounds one of the cave goblins found here. Apparantely, some years ago a young man and his friend were visiting the cave when they saw a flash of light. The man pointed his camera at where the light was and he suddenly disappeared. When the young man's body was found the only image left on his camera was that of a goblin. Cheddar caves still receives many hundreds of enquiries each year asking whether this creature is real or not. See the picture on the front cover of this book and make your own mind up.

There is of course much more to Cheddar Caves & Gorge including exhibitions and attractions. Situated in Britain's biggest and most stunning gorge which comprises a 1,000 acre nature reserve and 400ft towering limestone cliffs, it is easily one of the best days out for all the family that you are likely to find.

# - mines an iron ore -

## FLORENCE MINE
**Florence Mine Heritage
Centre, Egremont, Cumbria
Tel: 01946 825830**

Located between the Lake District fells
and the Cumbrian Coast, Florence Mine
Heritage Centre is based at the last,
deep Iron ore mine in Western Europe.
Here you will find the story of
'haematite', a top quality Iron Ore that
was mined here on a significant scale,
and although it is found in a variety of
different forms, the red of the ore has
become the distinctive colour of the
mine - hence the miners being referred
to as the 'Red Men' of Cumbria. This is
a fully working mine and is a great day
out.

*Top Left - the spectacular Gough's Cave at
Cheddar Caves and Gorge and (middle left),
the remains of Cheddar Man. Bottom left
and right - Florence Mine, the last deep
working Iron Ore mine in Europe.*

## ROYSTON CAVE
**Melbourn Street, Royston,
Hertfordshire
Tel: 01763 245484**

There are numerous medieval carvings, mostly of pagan origin, on the walls of this circular bell-shaped chamber but the exact meaning behind them remains a mystery to this day. It is believed that the cave may have been used by the Knights Templar as the sect held a weekly market at Royston between 1199 and 1254. The cave would have provided a cool store for their produce. It was in 1742 that the rediscovery of the cave occurred when a long forgotten shaft was discovered by 2 workmen digging a hole.

## BEER QUARRY CAVES
**Quarry Lane, Beer,
near Seaton, Devon
Tel: 01297 680282**

Thousands of pick marks from Roman quarrymen can still be seen even after more than 2,000 years at these caves. The caves are named after the nearby town of Beer and are a very old quarry that provided stones for the construction of Westminster Abbey, Windsor Castle, and the Tower of London. In fact Beer Quarry has supplied stone for about 24 cathedrals. They were extensively mined by the Romans and it is thought that they could even have been mined during the Stone Age.

The caves are regularly used for hibernating by Bechstein's Bats which is one of the rarest bats in Britain. Many other species of bat also regularly occupy the caves.

*Beer Quarry Caves.*

## INGLEBOROUGH CAVE
**Clapham, North Yorkshire
Tel: 01524 251242**

An impressive network of sculpted passages and shafts can be seen at Ingleborough Cave which until discovered in 1837 had remained hidden behind calcite dams. You can explore up to half a kilometre into the mountain and new discoveries continue to be made to this day.

## STUMP CROSS CAVERNS
**Greenhow Hill, Pateley
Bridge, Harrogate,
North Yorkshire
Tel: 01756 752780**

Stump Cross Caverns formed millions of years ago but was not discovered until 1860 by miners. The remains of wolverines (a giant member of the weasel family) have been discovered here and there are many interesting sections of the caverns to explore, each amusingly named.

## AULD REEKIE TOURS
**45 Niddry Street, Edinburgh**
**Tel: 0131 557 4700**

Edinburgh has a gory and quite terrifying past that most visitors would be unaware of - were it not for Auld Reekie Tours, one of the oldest tour operators of this type in the city. The Underground Vaults tour takes you into the old town below South Bridge which is said to be one of the most actively haunted places for paranormal activity in the world. Don't just take our word for it, this tour has been featured on 'Scariest Places in the World' hosted by Linda Blair of 'The Exorcist' fame. Working pagan temples, cannibals, plague, graverobbers, myths and legends, and a whole lot more will you see and learn about from your costumed guides. The dark side of Edinburgh is fully revealed and Mary King's Close in particular will shock you. Many have fled here in sheer terror.

Thousands of supernatural sightings and occurences have been reported from the areas you will visit on your underground trip and to cap it off you will witness the horrible pain and suffering endured by many at the Torture Museum, which has some pretty gruesome torture instruments. Highly recommended.

## MERCAT TOURS
**28 Blair Street, Edinburgh**
**Tel: 0131 225 5445**

Another longstanding grisly tour operator in Edinburgh is Mercat Tours. They offer a whole variety of tours themed on the creepy, macabre, or downright horrific including their Murder & Mystery, Ghosts & Ghouls, and Ghost Hunter Trail tours. In addition to these, and as with Auld Reekie Tours, you can sample the delights of the supernatural on the Mary King's Close tour  This is a place where pestilence, fire and plague have all left their mark. During the time of the plague Mary King's Close was a squalid, crowded neighbourhood that was rife with disease. Thousands were killed for being 'witches' including many of their 'evil' pets. Cats and dogs by the thousands were burned alive along with their owners and, with the cat and dog populations depleted, there were no predators left to kill the rats which carried and spread the plague like wildfire. In 1645 the government of Edinburgh decided to quarantine all Edinburgh's plague victims into Mary King's Close. They were locked in and left to die despite all their anguished screams for food, water, and mercy. Left until the screams could be heard no more, about a third of the population of the city died that year.

They say some things should be left buried forever and if you could hear the testimonies of the numerous people who have experienced strange happenings on this tour, I doubt you would want to ever consider taking it. Cold touches on the face, head and arms, rapid changes in temperature, and even spectral manifestations are all reported phenomena experienced by previous participants of this tour. The hidden underground vaults also have a shocking tale to tell. These are grim and ghastly places where Edinburgh's genuine historic underground city is revealed to you.

Having operated since 1985, Mercat Tours have entertained hundreds of thousands of visitors on their conducted tours over the years. It can be said with all honesty that they operate one of the most atmospheric and genuinely tension-filled tour that you are ever likely to take. Be afraid. Be very afraid.

## KENTS CAVERN
**Ilsham Road, Wellswood,**
**Torquay, Devon**
**Tel: 01803 215136**

Beatrix Potter visited here in 1893 and Agatha Christie referred to Kents Cavern in her 1924 novel, The Man in the Brown Suit. Recognised as the most important Palaeolithic cave system in Britain, the caves were extensively excavated during the last few centuries and stalagmite floors were carefully removed to reveal a plethora of items that dated from over 500,000 years ago to the end of the last Ice Age, 12,500 years ago. The limestone rock surrounding the caves was formed during the Devonian period some 385 million years ago when this part of the world lay beneath the sea, south of the equator.

Whilst Kents Cavern is justifiably famous as having some of the most beautiful and stunning natural underground architecture to be found anywhere, it is also the place that established the reputation of William Pengelly, the most notable paleontologist of his time and the first man to provide evidence supporting Charles Darwin's theory of evolution. It was Pengelly who oversaw the excavation of the stalagmite floor of Kents Cavern and subsequently discovered a multitude of animal remains that were to astound people of the time. In addition to hyena horse and bison bones, he was to discover the bones and fossils of extinct giants such as the sabre-tooth tiger, mammoth, and woolly rhinoceros. Human bones were also discovered and modern dating methods meant that in 1988, the human jaw bone that was originally unearthed in 1927 was radio-carbon dated, subsequently being identified as belonging to a type of 'modern' human being who would have occupied the cave in Torquay some 31,000 years ago. This amazing discovery represented the first conclusive proof that Modern man took over from Neanderthal man. Another find at Kents Cavern was a massive tooth which weighed 7 pounds. It belonged to a prehistoric mammoth and was found near the caves entrance.

A guided tour of Kents Cavern takes visitors into a maze of tunnels and illuminated grottoes. It is amazing to think that man lived here in the Ice Age and that these were occupied tens of thousands of years ago. Some of the finds discovered here can now be seen at the Torquay Museum including a crude hand axe made of stone. It is about 300,000 years old and is one of the oldest man-made implements ever found in Britain.

The caves are also home to some of the most spectacular stalactite and stalagmite formations in the country. Just to remind you, a stalactite comes down and a stalagmite grows up. Quite beautiful and stunning, seeing these formations is a wonderful experience as are the mysterious geological rock formations scattered throughout the caves. Daytime tours are led and interpreted by expert guides who will amaze you with some of the facts. When I last visited the caves, halfway through the tour the lights went out. Pitch blackness. Part of the tour maybe, or Ice Age man letting you know your on his property. Who knows, it may just be an oversight on that outstanding electricity bill.

*Mysterious and haunting. A guided tour of the labyrinthine passages and illuminated grottoes that were occupied tens of thousands of years ago is a stirring experience at Kents Cavern. The caves are so important to the history of Britain and ancient Britons that they are classified as the oldest Scheduled Ancient Monument in Britain.*

# - follies & fred flintstone -

## HAWKSTONE PARK AND FOLLIES

**Hawkstone Park,
Weston-under-Redcastle,
Shrewsbury, Shropshire
Tel: 01939 200611**

Created in the 18th century by Sir Rowland Hill and his son Richard, Hawkstone Park and Follies became one of the finest historic parklands in Europe. Covering over 100 acres, there are ravines, arches and bridges, intricate pathways, concealed grottos, towers and unusual monuments, and secret tunnels. King Arthur addressing his troops in the awesome caves and the hermit in his hermitage can also be seen at this remarkable place.

Such is the size of Hawkstone Park that it even has a large hotel, restaurant, and 2 golf courses.

## HOLY AUSTIN ROCK HOUSES

**Kinver Edge, Kinver,
near Stourbridge,
West Midlands
Tel: 01384 872553**

Kinver Edge is home to the last troglodyte dwellings to be occupied in England and these unique rock houses are carved into a contorted sandstone ridge. Remarkably, they were inhabited right up to the 1950's and have since been restored to their 19th century heyday. Standing at the impressive frontage you almost expect Fred Flintstone to come out and greet you. The on-site curator's house is half house/half cave but I doubt he complains as the area is covered in woodland and heath, boasting quite dramatic views over the surrounding counties.

*Not a grotty grotto but a great grotto at Hawkstone Park and Follies.*

*Holy Austin Rock Houses, the last troglodyte dwellings to be occupied in England.*

## CHISLEHURST CAVES
**Old Hill, Chislehurst, Kent**
**Tel: 0208 467 3264**

Enter a labyrinth of over 20 miles of mysterious dark tunnels and caverns that were hewn from the chalk beneath Chislehurst. This vast complex was originally carved out over a period of 8,000 years in the search for flint and chalk, and it is divided into 3 main sections; Saxon, Druid, and Roman.

Chalk has long been important to many civilisations and was used in lime burning and brick-making. Flint, of course, was used to fire tinderboxes and flintlock guns. The caves have also seen use as an ammunitions depot during the 1914 World War, and the deepest air-raid shelter outside London protecting 15,000 people every night during the Blitz.

## WHITE SCAR CAVE
**Ingleton, North Yorkshire**
**Tel: 00524 241244**

Discovered by a student named Christopher Long in 1923, White Scar Cave is said to be the longest show cave in Britain and an extended tour takes the visitor past cascading waterfalls. The cave takes its name from the limestone outcrops or scars which overlook the entrance, and certainly the highlight of any visit will be the 200,000 year old Battlefield Cavern. At over 330ft long with the roof 100ft high in places, this is one of the largest caverns in Britain and it has thousands of stalactites which hang in great clusters from the roof. There are also curious cave formations including the Arum Lily and the Devil's Tongue.

## CRESSWELL CRAGS
**Crags Road, Welbeck,**
**Worksop, Nottinghamshire**
**Tel: 01909 720 378**

Cresswell Crags is a limestone gorge that is liberally sprinkled with caves and small fissures. Prehistoric tools and animal remains found in the caves provide evidence of occupation during the last Ice Age, and a more recent find is the discovery of Britain's only known Ice Age rock art. Exhibitions, cave tours, walks around the beautiful gorge, and special events are all exciting things to see and do at Cresswell Crags, one of the key sites of archeological heritage in Europe.

## CLEARWELL CAVES - ANCIENT IRON MINES
**near Coleford, Royal Forest of Dean, Gloucestershire**
**Tel: 01594 832535**

Clearwell Caves are situated in an area of superb natural beauty in a mining region where iron has been extracted for thousands of years. You can discover a new world here beneath the Royal Forest of Dean and see how iron ore has been mined from this quite stunning cave system. There are 9 big caverns to explore, and you have the opportunity to purchase crystals, minerals and ochres.

Mining is now believed to have begun in the Forest of Dean during the Mesolithic Period (Middle Stone Age), and small scale mining carries on here today using traditional techniques, many of which would have been used by the earliest miners.

## WINSTON CHURCHILL'S BRITAIN AT WAR EXPERIENCE
**64-66 Tooley Street, London SE1. Tel: 0207 403 3171**

This is your opportunity to experience what life was like in the London Blitz during the most turbulent period in the history of the 20th century - the Second World War. Winston Churchill's Britain at War Experience recreates the sites, sounds, and even the chaos that ensued following an air raid warning. In fact you can take the lift to the London Underground air raid shelter, a place where thousands spent sleepless nights following the dreaded wail of the air raid siren.

This really is a superb exhibition that uses authentic documents and artifacts to illustrate the story. The Anderson shelter, Drury Lane dressing room, and Rainbow Corner which entertained GI's are all worth seeing. Learn about the Land Army Girls who fought battles on the Home Front or stroll along the recreated little shops of Southwark and see the prices of goods in 'old money' (pounds, shillings and pence).

Other exhibits at this first class attraction include the underground cinema where authentic wartime news is screened, the BBC radio studio where the latest messages from Churchill, Chamberlain, Roosevelt and Hitler can be heard, and real wartime bombs, documents and photography in the Bomb Disposal display. You can also see how people coped with everyday food and clothing rationing, view gas masks and ration books, and see the anxiety and anticipation of evacuees as they waited patiently to be transported to new homes.

Specifically designed to tie in with the National Curriculum, special 'dressing-up' sessions for school parties includes gasmasks, tin helmets, and 1940's clothing and uniforms. School was never so much fun in my day.

## CABINET WAR ROOMS
**Clive Steps, King Charles Street, London SW1A Tel: 0207 930 6961**

Near the corner of St.James's Park, where Birdcage Walk meets Horse Guards Road, a barely noticeable sign points you in the direction of the Cabinet War Rooms. It is here, in this huge network of rooms, that Winston Churchill, his Cabinet, his War Cabinet, and his intelligence advisors spent much of the Second World War.

Work began in June 1938 to adapt these former storage areas which are 10ft below ground, and their hurried construction was a result of lessons learned during the First World War and the advent of the bomber. They were built to withstand the Nazi Blitzkrieg as RAF planners implied that some 600 tons of bombs would rain down on the capital in just the very first week of a war, causing 200,000 casualties.

Churchill's own room where he slept when it was too dangerous to return to Downing Street can be seen, as can the Cabinet Room, Map Room, Transatlantic Telephone Room, and numerous others. One feature is The Tunnel which visitors walk through. It is a hole drilled through a 5 metre square block of concrete which was previously a room filled in to prevent collapse by bombing. You almost expect Churchill's cigar smoke to waft by you.

## CASTLETON CAVERNS
comprising:

### - BLUE JOHN CAVERN
**Castleton, Hope Valley,
Derbyshire. Tel: 01433 620638**

### - SPEEDWELL CAVERN
**Winnats Pass, Castleton,
Hope Valley, Derbyshire
Tel: 01433 620512**

### - TREAK CLIFF CAVERN
**Castleton, Hope Valley,
Derbyshire. Tel: 01433 620571**

### - PEAK CAVERN
**Castleton, Hope Valley,
Derbyshire. Tel: 01433 620285**

The Castleton Caverns comprise the 4 caverns as listed above, each of which have a special appeal in their own right.

Blue John Cavern is world famous and is home to 8 of the 14 known varieties of Blue John Stone. The mineral has been mined here for centuries and is a beautiful ornamental fluor-spar that is widely sought after by collectors for its subtle colouration, which has wide-ranging shades. The name was given to it in the 18th century by 2 miners, Joseph Hall and John Kirk, to distinguish it from 'Black Jack', the local name for Zinc Blende. Visitors here can see the Variegated Cavern, the Waterfall Cavern, the Grand Crystallised Cavern, and Lord Mulgraves Dining Room where his Lordship entertained miners, and where fine veins of Blue John can be seen in their natural state in the limestone.

Speedwell Cavern is a mine with several natural chambers and an underground canal where you step onto a tour boat. From here you glide silently through the workings of a 200 year old lead mine. The boat lands about 200 metres below the surface of the hill and you emerge into a stunning cavern containing the awesome Bottomless Pit - a gigantic subterranean lake.

Treak Cliff Cavern has superb stalagmite and stalactite formations that can be seen at this old mine which was used mainly to mine Blue John. In 1926 miners broke through into natural caverns beyond, and there are some splendid sights that today's visitor can see. See the miniature grottoes of Fairyland, the Dream Cave, the Witches Cave, and veins of Blue John Stone.

Peak Cavern is the only wholly natural cave of the 4 and was known to locals as the Devil's Arse. The approach and entry is one of the most stunning and memorable sights in Britain and, indeed, is the largest natural cave entrance in the British Isles. Just inside the vast funnel-like entrance is the site of the old cavern ropeworks. The Orchestral Chamber, the Devil's Staircase, and Pluto's Dining Room are all worth seeing here.

*Blue John Stone in its natural state
can be seen at Blue John Cavern.*

# - cable cars to lead mines -

## HEIGHTS OF ABRAHAM
**Matlock Bath, Derbyshire**
**Tel: 01629 582365**

Traditionally, lead has been mined in the vicinity of Masson Hill since Roman times, and the Heights of Abraham which is high on the southern slopes of Masson Hill has many caverns which were all originally lead mines. Hundreds of years of concentrated lead mining in the area ended late in the 18th century and areas of Masson Hill looked like an industrial wasteland. In 1780 part of the southern slopes were enclosed and trees and shrubs planted to develop an estate known as the Heights of Abraham. This name was used because of the similarity to the heights below Quebec which General Wolfe and his troops scaled in 1759.

In 1844 the Masson Cavern was opened to the public and the Victoria Prospect Tower was built to provide work for the many unemployed lead miners, but by the late 1970's the once grand landscaped gardens had become seriously dilapidated. In 1978 restoration work began to conserve this unique place, and 1984 saw the commissioning of the first alpine-style cable car system in Britain. This saved visitors the punishing climb to the top of the Heights, and together with the new Treetops Visitor Centre once again established the Heights of Abraham as a prestige visitor attraction.

The cable cars are a great way to enjoy the panoramic views of Derbyshire on your 568 metre climb from the base to the top station. The journey is a vertical rise of 169 metres passing over 4 towers, the highest tower being located over the sheer face of Long Tor escarpment.

The famous show caverns here illustrate perfectly what it would have been like to be a 17th century lead miner. Great Masson Cavern portrays the story of how the caverns were formed and you walk through underground passageways deep inside the rock before discovering the Great Chamber. The Great Rutland Cavern - Nestus Mine is an experience of a day in the life of a lead mining family. It is not so long ago that hurricane lamps and candles would have been used to illuminate the visitor's way through these great caverns but today's visitor, in a properly lit environment, can see a variety of minerals such as malachite, fluor-spar and calcite.

Coffee shop, bar and restaurant, gift shops, and ample picnic areas are all here at this quality attraction.

## WILLIAMSON'S TUNNELS
**15-17 Chatham Place,
Liverpool, Merseyside
Tel: 0151 475 9833**

Most people would be unaware of Williamson's Tunnels but this labyrinth of tunnels and caverns under the Edge Hill district of Liverpool has a quite fascinating - if somewhat strange - tale to tell. This unusual underground kingdom was built during the first few decades of the 1800's under the guidance of retired tobacco merchant Joseph Williamson, and the exact purpose of their construction is still not known for certain.

Around 1805 Joseph Williamson and his wife moved into a property at Mason Street, Edge Hill, and this would be their home for the rest of their lives. The area was largely undeveloped and although the houses had cellars, Williamson thought they should follow the current trend and have large gardens behind them. New houses under construction had a certain amount of space behind them, but a 20ft drop to the street behind, so to accommodate the new gardens Williamson had his men build brick arches so they could be extended onto. The first parts of these noteworthy tunnels were now in place.

The manner in which matters subsequently developed is the subject of much speculation. The severity of the recession and soldiers returning from war meant Williamson had an abundance of manpower available, and he kept taking more and more men on. Underground, the men worked by candlelight, often performing pointless tasks. There is evidence that arches were built and immediately bricked up again. Some arches and tunnels lead nowhere. Oddly, Williamson died on 1st May, 1940, a day that would subsequently become International Workers Day. The tunneling stopped immediately and was never resumed. Find out much more on a visit here.

## WESTERN APPROACHES
**1 Rumford Street (under Derby House), Liverpool, Merseyside
Tel: 0151 227 2008**

Consisting of over 100 secret underground rooms that comprise around 50,000sq.ft of bunker area, the gas-proof and bomb-proof Western Approaches complex is known as the 'citadel' or 'fortress', and it is here that the Battle of the Atlantic was masterminded and the hunting down of the Bismark was conducted. The Royal Navy, Royal Marines and Air Force, worked jointly to monitor enemy convoys and 'wolf-packs' of submarines which were threatening Britain during the early part of the war.

Visitors here can see the main Operations Room where giant maps were used for plotting vessels journeys, the Cinema Room to view archive footage, the Tele-printer Room where messages were received, and the Decoding Room where translation of codes took place before relaying the information to air and sea forces in the Atlantic. The Enigma De-coding Machine, recovered from a sinking U-Boat, was kept in the Decoding Room. There is much more to see at Western Approaches which has a 7ft thick roof and 3ft thick walls.

## DOVER CASTLE SECRET WARTIME TUNNELS
**Dover Castle, Dover, Kent**
**Tel: 01304 211067**

Discover life as it was, deep in the labyrinth of tunnels located in the White Cliffs of Dover beneath historic Dover Castle. The castle has the most massive tower in Britain; an almost 100ft cube with walls that are up to 21ft thick, and the castle sits in a commanding position on top of the high cliffs on the site of an ancient Saxon fortification. The tunnels were originally constructed during the Napoleonic Wars and then used again in World War Two as an underground hospital and numerous offices.

The war against Napoleon in 1797 required huge numbers of soldiers to be found quarters in the town. Miners were brought in to create 7 tunnels to be used as barracks, and by 1803 over 2,000 men were using the tunnels as living quarters. They even had fireplaces built in. The Dunkirk evacuation of May 1940 was directed from within these tunnels, and enemy aircraft were tracked from within the offices here.

## POLDARK MINE
**Wendron, Helston, Cornwall**
**Tel: 01326 573173**

Set in the picturesque Wendron Valley, Poldark Mine dates from about 1730 and was worked until 1810, after which it was closed. By the 1940's all trace of the mine had gone and it was only rediscovered by accident when the site was purchased in 1966. The land then was marshy and boggy, and when drained, the new owners discovered a long forgotten mine underneath their feet. Today, visitors can take a guided underground tour of the recreated Poldark Mine and walk in the footsteps of 18th century Cornish tin miners. There is also much more to see and do here as attractions include a museum, craft workshops, and plenty of entertainment for children.

## CHARLESTOWN SHIPWRECK, RESCUE & HERITAGE CENTRE
**Quay Road, Charlestown,**
**Cornwall. Tel: 01726 69897**

Located in an historic china clay building, visitors here can gain a fascinating insight into the history of Charlestown and shipwrecks. In fact the shipwreck and recovered historical items on display in the centre represent the largest private collection of this type on public display in Europe. A vast collection of items is on show recovered from over 150 shipwrecks from all parts of the globe. Wonder if they've got my mobile phone I lost when my rowing boat got waterlogged on the boating lake last summer?

After enjoying the shipwreck collection, diving memorabilia, Cornish mining artifacts, and various other interesting collections, visitors can walk through underground tunnels where clay trucks were pushed out to the ships in port. This is one of the most unusual and stimulating places in the south-west of the country to visit.

# KING ARTHUR'S LABYRINTH

**Corris, Machynlleth, Powys, Mid Wales. Tel: 01654 761584**

King Arthur's Labyrinth is situated in the old Braichgoch Slate Mines at Corris. This most unusual visitor attraction takes you on an exciting boat ride along a subterranean river deep into the spectacular caverns under the Braichgoch mountain, passing through a magical waterfall and into the Labyrinth. Thereafter a walk through the caverns to learn about the legends of King Arthur, the wizard Merlin and Avalon, is a journey you will long remember. This is one of the most mysterious and legendary stories that Wales has to tell and the surroundings greatly add to the mystery and wonder.

Audio-visual tableaux relate the Arthurian legends including one that says King Arthur still sleeps in a cave in the Welsh hills awaiting the call to rescue the 'Cymru' when in danger again. Stories from the Mabinogion and the Tales of Taliesin form part of the King Arthur theme here as you listen to the story of the boy Myrddin who talks to a king called Gwrtheyrn, the battle between the red and white dragons, the legend of Bran's head, the voyage to Avalon, and the battle with the giant Rhitta amongst others. The stunning light and sound effects makes the experience all the more interesting, indeed enchanting.

Your journey ends with a return trip along the subterranean river into the grounds of Corris Craft Centre where books and gifts based on the Celtic Arthurian theme can be purchased in the gift shop. Visitors are also invited to see the various skills of the craft workers making pottery, jewellery, candles, etc.

Myths and legends have long been associated with King Arthur who is said to have come out of the darkness to defeat the powerful Saxon invaders. His feats of bravery and supernatural powers were related by bards and story-tellers, subsequently passed on from generation to generation. Perhaps we may never discover the truth behind the Arthurian legends but a visit here will certainly increase your speculation.

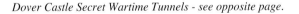

*Dover Castle Secret Wartime Tunnels - see opposite page.*

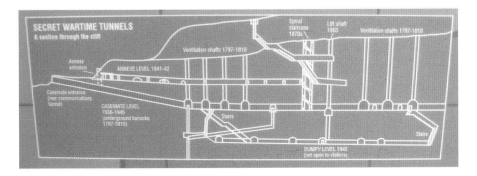

# - don't by pass the baths -

## WELWYN ROMAN BATHS
**Welwyn by-pass, Welwyn, Hertfordshire**
**Tel: 01707 271362**

This site shows the remains of a 3rd century Roman bathing suite, the only surviving feature of a Roman villa built over 1,700 years ago. It is ingeniously preserved in a vault under the A1 (M) at Welwyn by-pass and provides a fascinating insight into how the Romans bathed. There are a series of hot and cold rooms, and you can also see how the 'hypocaust' under-floor heating would have worked and where slaves would have sat for hours on end tending to the system and stoking the fire.

The discovery of the site is both interesting and fascinating. A series of panels illustrate how the site was uncovered by archaeologists, and there are displays of finds from the villa which help to understand how people lived and worked in the Roman countryside.

Welwyn Roman Baths have somewhat limited opening times, although groups are welcome by appointment at most times. This is a particularly entertaining and aducational place for children to visit, and an experienced guide provides an informative talk on the villa and Baths together with worksheets for school parties.

You won't see Caesar and you won't have many laughs, but you will learn a lot at the Welwyn Roman Baths.

# Part Two
## - USA -

*Crystal Shrine Grotto, constructed of rock quartz, crystal and
semi-precious stones, is a wonderful depiction of Christ's
time on earth, from birth to the resurrection - page 60.*

# GROTTO OF THE REDEMPTION
## West Bend, Iowa,

Records broken here as The Grotto of the Redemption is not only the largest grotto in the world but also the largest collection of minerals and fossils in one place in the world. Startingly, it covers an entire city block.

This vast complex was constructed by Father Paul Dobberstein who, after becoming ill with pneumonia, prayed to the Blessed Virgin Mary (the Mother of God) that if his health were restored he would build a shrine in her honour. He subsequently recovered from his illness and went to West Bend as a pastor. For over a decade he stockpiled rocks and precious stones and in 1912 set about working on his shrine. The many curious visitors who came to see his work left donations to assist costs, and he was so overcome that he decided to build a whole complex that would depict man's fall, to his subsequent redemption by Christ. It took him 42 years until he died in 1954. What visitors see is not a single grotto but 9, each portraying a scene in the life of Christ. Frequently described as a miracle in stone the artistry has to be seen to be believed. Many consider it to be the 'Eighth Wonder of the World'.

## KOKOPELLI'S CAVE BED & BREAKFAST
**3204 Crestridge Drive,
Farmington, New Mexico**

Now here's a strange one. Featured on a host of television programmes such as CNN News, CBS Morning Show, the Oprah Winfrey Show, and written about in numerous magazines and newspapers, Kokopelli's Cave Bed & Breakfast is quite unique in the world. Whilst there may be other cave or underground dwellings offering accommodation, there is surely none quite like this.

Kokopelli's is not a natural cave as it was blasted out in 1980. It was originally the intention for it to be a geologic office for consulting geologist Bruce Black, but by 1997 when it was ready for use after ventilation holes, drilling, electrical lines and everything else was complete, it was decided to use the cave to offer bed and continental breakfast. The cave itself is 70ft below the surface of the ground and is accessed via the entrance which is in the cliff face. You then walk down a sloping path, descend a ladder, and finally reach Kokopelli's unusual place. Consisting of 1,650 sq.ft of space, this bizarre cave home was dynamited and carved out of a 65 million year old sandstone formation that sits 280ft above the La Plata River. From the cave and the cliff tops there are amazing views over 4 states.

Surprisingly, this is an upmarket cave dwelling for the discerning person. A well appointed kitchen, hot tub, plush carpeting, and hot and cold running water are all here to be seen at this luxury cliff dwelling. Located north of Farmington, New Mexico, near the well known Mesa Verde National Monument, Kokopelli's is a bit off the beaten track but it has to be seen to be believed.

## OLD NEWGATE PRISON & COPPER MINE
**115 Newgate Road,
East Granby, Connecticut**

This is one of the very best tourist attractions to be found in Connecticut and is a good insight into how harsh conditions could be in 18th century American prisons and reform centres.

Old Newgate Mine opened early in the 18th century as America's first chartered copper mine. As much larger copper deposits were found shortly after in New Mexico, Utah, Arizona, and other states, the mine soon became unprofitable and was closed. A few years later the Colony of Connecticut made plans for the tunnels to be converted for use as a state prison, and as it was very secure the General Assembly decided it was perfect to incarcerate serious criminals such as counterfeiters, robbers and horse thieves in a secure and working environment. Alternatives to prison were the whipping post and sometimes torture or hanging.

The first prisoner held here was John Hinson who was committed for burglary, although he was also the first to escape from the prison, and during the Revolutionary War many Loyalists were imprisoned here. There is much to see in the cramped, low tunnels, and the former guardhouse contains a small museum which illustrates the history of the site.

## FORESTIERE UNDERGROUND GARDENS
**5021 West Shaw Avenue, Fresno, California**

This amazing cave house and underground complex was the result of 40 years work by Baldasare Forestiere, a Sicilian immigrant. The astonishing results of his hand-sculpted and designed subterranean paradise include a chapel and garden, an underground garden home complete with library, fish pond and aquarium, and a network of passageways, courtyards, niches and rooms numbering over 100. An auto-tunnel which runs the length of the gardens is almost 800ft long. Foriestiere's achievements are all the more remarkable as he used only ordinary hand tools and a wheelbarrow to complete his project. All the areas are adorned with a unique variety of trees including pomegranate, mulberry, chinese date, walnut, pear, olive, lemon and orange.

Tradition is important in Italy, and in Sicily, when the father of a household dies, the oldest son inherits everything. Although Baldasare's family were quite wealthy, he could work all his life and receive nothing when his father passed away. As his eldest brother would inherit the family estate, Baldasare decided to go to America to work and buy his own land. At his first American job he had learned tunneling techniques working on New York City's aqueduct system, and later moved to Fresno to buy land with the intention of opening a citrus plantation. Unfortunately the land proved to be solid rock underneath the topsoil and unsuitable for farming. One day he found himself sitting in his cellar room in the 120 degrees heat of the California Central Valley. Noticing the sun shining through the skylight he wondered if he could get a tree to grow underground. He tried, succeeded, and planted another. That also grew and this was to be the beginning of the Forestiere Underground Gardens.

Baldasare has said that at that time he had great visions in his mind which overwhelmed him. Over the next 40 years he would dig, dig, and dig again, excavating scores of rooms and fashioning an underground wonderland of such complexity that after his death scientists, architects and engineers from all over the world acclaimed him as an engineering genius.

Working on neighbouring farms to subsidise his ever growing cave house complex, Baldasare expanded his underground home by adding room after room, each one having an opening in the ceiling for light and fresh air. He planted a fruit tree under many of the openings where it would be watered by the rain, whilst openings in the house could be closed by windows in the

*A citrus tree flourishes in the unique setting of Forestiere Underground Gardens in Fresno, California.*

event of heavier rainfalls. This mans love of fruit trees (perhaps a reminder of Sicily) saw him plant numerous varieties, with some of the trees grafted to bear more than one type of fruit. Some trees even had 3 grafts and it is believed that yet another tree had an incredible 7 different types of citrus. As above ground citrus trees were prone to frost, but it is not a problem for underground trees, Baldasare would never go hungry.

Some passageways were made narrow for the air to move faster, or were curved to advance or slow the breeze. Most passageways were slightly inclined to enable water flow, and sump pits were strategically placed to prevent flooding. Baldasare reasoned that the hot air needed to be dispersed quickly so he made the skylights narrow at the top and wide at the bottom. In this way he used convections and thermal syphons as hot air rises and

cold air sinks. The sheer variety and abundance of fruit trees - some of which are quite rare - that flourished in this underground world was quite unbelievable. Some are planted as much as 22ft below ground level.

Hardpan, cement and mortar has been used throughout the complex for textural variety in addition to structural purposes. Roman arches, sculptures, domes, columns, ornate niches, pergolas adorned with cascading grapevines, recessed seating, and a plethora of other delightful touches were added.

Extending over 4 hectares this most unique cave house and underground wonderland is now listed on the National Register of Historic Places. Visitors from all parts of the world have been enchanted by seeing and admiring the results of a single man's labours which took him 40 years, having nothing but basic tools and a vision to fulfill.

## NIAGARA CAVE
**29842 County Road, Harmony, Minnesota**

Niagara Cave is one of the most interesting and unique geological attractions in the area and is also one of the Midwest's largest limestone caverns. There are numerous notable sights here such as a 60ft high waterfall, the Stalactite Room which holds a multitude of colourful rock formations in a massive chamber, exposed fossils that date to over 400 million years old, a wishing well, echo chamber, and an weird sight called Paul Bunyan's Bed. The most unusual attraction here has to be the Wedding Chapel. About 500 wedding ceremonies have been performed here although why anyone would wish to be joined to their spouse in a morbid cave is speculative.

At a constant 48 degrees all year round Niagara Cave is quite pleasant to visit. It has previously been voted as one of the top 10 caves in the United States and there is certainly plenty of interesting things to see and do here. Picnic grounds covering 10 acres, a chance to try your luck at mining for real gemstones and fossils, and an informative guided tour are all part of the fun of a day out at Niagara Cave.

## BRIDAL CAVE
**Camdenton, Missouri**

Another cave where you can tie the knot, this time in Missouri and a lot more commercialised. Local folklore tells of the legendary and fascinating tale of the Indian Wedding ceremony held in the cave in the early 1800's. This is how the cave came to be named Bridal Cave and since that time it has subsequently held about 2,000 underground weddings, which is said to be a world record. Apparently people come from all over the world to be married here.

The cave's temperature is a constant 60 degrees so 'something blue' for the bride should not be flannelette knickers. Your romantic Bridal Cave wedding consists of a private dressing area upon arrival before availing yourselves of one of the 2 tantalising wedding packages. Package 'A', the 'Sweetheart Special', offers the use of the stalacpipe adorned chapel, recorded pipe organ music, a minister to perform your ceremony, a lifetime pass to the cave for bride and groom (what!), and 2 gold rimmed toasting glasses with a bottle of sparkling cider. The last known quote for that little lot was $400 or so. If you really want to push the boat out then Package 'B', the 'Romance to Remember' option, offers all of the above plus silk or fresh flowers for bride and groom, and the services of a professional photographer which includes 15 colour prints in an embossed album and an 8 x 10 inch wall portrait. The last we heard this option came in at $550. Take your pick.

Bridal Cave say they "look forward to making your dream come true" and that "the memories of this special day will be treasured for a lifetime". Surely weddings should be bright and breezy church affairs with your photos taken out in the sunshine afterwards. Funerals or wakes are more appropriate to be held underground. Oh well, to coin a phrase; "it takes all sorts to make a world" I suppose. By the way, Bridal cave is said to contain more onyx formations than any other showcave. Maybe that's the attraction.

## UNDERGROUND RACQUETS LTD
**1331 Cuvuk War Road, Carthage, Missouri**

Never mind Wimbledon, how about playing tennis underground in a huge limestone cavern. The benefits are obvious; rain won't stop play and the temperature is steady whatever time of the year it is. Yes its unbelievable, but true. Underground Racquets Ltd operates this unusual sporting place which was up for rent after limestone quarrying ended. They have no overheads for heating or air-conditioning and membership levels are said to be on the increase. Unfortunately, as the club is for members only, you will have to ask in a very nice way if you want to take a look inside.

## MERAMEC CAVERNS
**Stanton, Missouri**

Meramec Caverns is quite a bizarre place with many claims to fame, probably the most noteworthy of which is the fact that it was used as a hideout for the infamous Jesse James and his band of outlaws. They used the caverns back in the early 1870's when his men and horses hid in the cave following the Gad's Hill train robbery. The history of the caverns can be traced back much further as although it was discovered in 1722 by Jacques Renault, a French miner, it was used for many years before that by local indians. From 1862 to 1864 the caverns were used for gunpowder manufacturing for the Civil War. The Union troops set up kilns and leaching vats in addition to building an underground railway station.

The caverns have an annual use for a quite unusual event; the world's only underground bodybuilding contest. Called 'Caveman', it is held in an impressive chamber of the caverns known as the 'Ballroom'. This chamber has been used for both public and private events since the end of the 19th century and is quite massive. It accommodates not only a stage but also 2,000 chairs.

The most impressive formation in the caverns is the 'Stage Curtain' found in a chamber named Theatre. This gargantuan frozen waterfall measures 21 metres high, 18 metres wide, and is 11 metres thick. It is estimated to be over 70 million years old and is said to be one of the largest cave formations in the world.

# - the blind ozarks cavefish -

## FANTASTIC CAVERNS
### 4872 N.Farm Road 125, Springfield, Missouri

More than living up to its name, this is one of almost 5,700 known caves scattered across the Missouri landscape, with more being discovered every year. Although only 20 or so of these caves are open to visitors this is one of the most impressive, and the only one to offer a riding tour - in unusual jeep-drawn trams.

Fantastic Caverns was discovered in 1862 by a dog belonging to a farmer. The dog had crawled through a crevice opening, and some years later the first proper exploration took place by 12 women from Springfield who had answered a newspaper

advertisement seeking explorers. The caverns showed no signs of previous habitation so it is likely their's were the first human footsteps ever to be heard there. However, a variety of animals have found a home at the caverns including the grotto salamander, the cave crayfish, and the rare, blind Ozarks cavefish. Clean, unpolluted water is essential for these creatures and, today, the water quality is very carefully monitored to ensure their survival.

The 55-minute tour of this ride-through cave is a journey back in time and the pleasant 60 degrees temperature makes it an enjoyable experience. Thousands of formations including stalactites, stalagmites, cave pearls, soda straws, delicate draperies, huge columns and more, can all be viewed in comfort.

*Your journey through the wondrous landscapes of Fantastic Caverns is made in jeep-drawn trams, to preserve its fragile beauty. The amazing and reclusive, blind Ozarks cavefish lives here, as do the grotto salamander and crayfish.*

## BRUNSON INSTRUMENT COMPANY
### East 23rd Street, Kansas City, Missouri

This entire 20,000sq metre factory is built underground in a limestone cliff that is covered by 300 million year old limestone.

It was A.N.Brunson who founded the Brunson Instrument Company in Kansas City, in traditional premises. Developing the business over the years, he realised that a completely stable environment was needed for the production of the fine optical and navigational instruments the company made. The revolutionary underground factory was the answer as it meant no building movement or traffic vibrations, top level security, and fine temperature and humidity control. Only the entrance is visible from the outside.

## HAUNTED CAVE
### Lewisburg, Ohio

Located 35 metres below ground in the tunnels of an abandoned limestone mine, every year this opens during the last weeks before Halloween when it is transformed into a fantastic and scary underground theme park. Tractor-drawn wagons take you into the mine and it is also home to over 30,000 Brown Bats, which can only add to the atmosphere.

## RADON HEALTH MINE
### 149 Depot Hill Road, Boulder, Montana

The Radon Mine was originally used as far back as 1924 for silver and lead ore mining. In 1949, the by then abandoned mine was found to have the presence of radioactivity, and a visiting woman (for the purpose of stock investment) discovered her ailment had disappeared. Word spread and soon this was turned into a radon-therapy mine. Low dose radiation therapy is said to be beneficial in easing a multitude of ailments and even pets are treated in the radon-laden air here. They advise you to bring a blanket and pillow if you would like to sleep. Whatever next.

## OLD SPANISH TREASURE CAVE
### Arkansas Highway 59, Sulphur Springs, Arkansas

The unsolved mystery of the legend of hidden treasure is ongoing at the Old Spanish Treasure Cave. It is believed that over 350 years ago Spanish Conquistador soldiers buried their treasure (today estimated to be worth over 40 million dollars) deep within the cavern. Gold coins, weapons, helmets and armour have been found, but despite numerous searches since 1885 the treasure-trove is still undiscovered.

# THE LOST SEA
**140 Lost Sea Road,
Sweetwater, Tennessee**

Quite remarkable, visitors here can take a guided tour on a glass bottomed boat over America's largest underground lake which covers almost 5 acres. It is recognized as a Registered National Landmark due to the abundance of rare anthodites (cave flowers).

Possibly the largest underground body of water in the world, The Lost Sea is part of an extensive cave system known as Craighead Caverns. They have been known and lived in since the days of the Cherokee Indians and a mile from the entrance is a chamber known as the Council Room. It is here that a large quantity of Indian artifacts such as arrowheads, pottery and weapons have been found, proving use of the cave by the Cherokees.

A Pleistocene jaguar's tracks and bones were found deep inside the caverns and some of the bones (discovered in 1939 and dating over 20,000 years old) are on display at the American Museum of Natural History in New York. During the Civil War the caves were mined by the Confederate Army for saltpetre which was used in the manufacture of gunpowder. A Union spy is said to have almost succeeded in blowing up the operation before he was discovered.

Throughout the early history of the caverns rumours persisted of a large underground lake located deep within here. It was not actually discovered until 1905 when a boy aged 13 managed to scramble through a very small opening 300ft underground. What the boy (Ben Sands) discovered was a gigantic room half filled with water that is now known as The Lost Sea.

# LOST WORLD CAVERNS
**Lewisburg, West Virginia**

This is a veritable wonderland of natural cave formations including stalactites and stalagmites, and features America's largest compound stalactite; the 30-ton 'Snowy Chandelier' which is said to be the world's best display of pure calcite. The Guiness World Record for stalagmite sitting (whatever next) was set in the Lost World Caverns in 1971 by Bobby Addis of Parkersburg, West Virginia. He sat at the top of the 28ft tall 'War Club' for 15 days, 23 hours, and 22 minutes. Wonder how he went to the toilet? If you think that's strange, what about the Weekly World News report in 1992 that claimed the caverns were home to 'Bat Boy', a large-eyed lad with demonic fangs who is said to have been raised in the darkness here by bats.

The caverns are entered through a long tunnel and the main cave is a huge chamber that is over 1,000ft long and 10 storeys high. Apart from the infamous War Club formation, visitors can see The Castle, The Bridal Veil, and Goliath formations, which are all notable sights.

When you emerge from the caverns, squinting in the sunlight, there is the regulation gift shop to visit and a small Natural History Museum adjacent. It has the biggest collection of dinosaur and fossil replicas in West Virginia - if that's a claim to fame.

# MYSTERY HILL
## 105 Haverhill Road, Salem, New Hampshire

Often compared to the English Stonehenge circle, Mystery Hill in New Hampshire was also built by ancient people who were knowledgeable in astronomy and stone construction. No one knows for certain who exactly built this American Stonehenge and inscriptions found throughout the site include Phoenician, Ogham, and Iberian Punic Script.

Mystery Hill, or America's Stonehenge, is probably the oldest megalithic (stone constructed) site in North America. It has been proved that the site is an accurate astronomically aligned calendar and it was - and still is - used to determine specific solar and lunar events each year. Cave-like primitive buildings, tunnels and low walls, are all spread over many acres of the hillside site of Mystery Hill. Unlike Stonehenge in England, the stones at Mystery Hill are much smaller. The largest is about 11 tons whereas the stones involved at Stonehenge are up to 45 tons each. Both sites have common points as they were in use as observatories and their many astronomical alignments include the summer solstice.

One of the main features of the Mystery Hill site is a huge flat stone resting on 4 small legs. Looking like a giant table, it has a groove around the edges that leads to a spout. The giant stone slab has been named the 'Sacrificial Stone' and it is reasonably certain that it was indeed used for this purpose; the groove and spout allowing the blood of the sacrifice to drain away. Underneath the Sacrificial Stone is an 8ft long shaft that leads to an underground chamber. Probably a priest would have been concealed in this chamber, speaking as if his were the voice of an oracle. To the crowd gathered around the sacrificial altar this would appear to be some kind of magic or the voice of a disembodied spirit.

There are numerous other caves and passages on the Mystery Hill site, the use of most being uncertain. Archaeological excavations at the site have unearthed a multitude of amazing items including prehistoric stone tools, pottery, manuscripts, and even manacles which were probably removed from slaves when this was a stop on the Railroad during the 1830's.

At over 4,000 years old, Mystery Hill still has many secrets yet to be discovered. Its maze of man-made chambers and ceremonial meeting places continue to astound visitors and perplex archaeologists. We may never know who built this site and we may never know who, or what, was sacrificed on the giant stone altar.

## COSMIC CAVERN
**6386 Highway 21 North,
Berryville, Arkansas**

Said to be the 'warmest' cave in the Ozarks with high humidity and a constant 62 degrees temperature, Cosmic Cavern is one of America's 'must-see' caves. Beautiful and unique formations here include helictites, draperies, flowstones, sodastraws, stalactites, stalagmites, and many other speleothems. An unusual and rare creature can sometimes be spotted within the striking cave formations; the Blind Ozarks Cave Salamander is in residence here.

The cavern contains 2 'bottomless' lakes which were discovered in 1845. The first, South Lake, has had trout swimming in it for over 50 years, although most of these have now gone blind and lost their colour. The end, or bottom, of both lakes has yet to be discovered despite attempts by many divers.

Another major attraction at Cosmic Cavern is the fairly recently discovered area called 'Silent Splendor'. Widely touted as a huge attraction in Arkansas, Silent Splendor houses one of the longest sodastraw formations in the Ozarks - an incredible 9ft. The Silent Splendor area has also been featured on CBS News and in newspapers all over the USA. It remains to this day one of the major cave finds in the region and is so picturesque and stunning that only a visit will do it justice.

There is much more to see and do at Cosmic Cavern including the unique opportunity to try your hand at gemstone panning. This is very similar to panning for gold except you are trying to discover sapphires, quartz, rubies, emeralds, and other precious stones. Any age group can participate and its great fun.

A pavillion, gift shop, museum, and a whole lot more all combine to make a great day out at Cosmic Cavern. Who knows, you may see the Blind Ozarks Cave Salamander, or even unearth a precious stone.

*The Ozarks is a physiographic and geologic highland region covering much of the Southern half of Missouri, an extensive portion of northern Arkansas, extending westward into southeast Kansas and northeastern Oklahoma.*

# CRYSTAL SHRINE GROTTO
## Memorial Park Cemetery, Memphis, Tennessee

This crystal cave made from natural rock, quartz, and semi-precious stones is carved out of a hillside and is entered through an opening in a large concrete, tree-stump looking mound found in Memorial Park Cemetery. As with the Grotto of the Redemption (see page 48) this is another shrine to Christ depicting from Birth to Resurrection. The cavern is also constructed of crystal and semi-precious stones and was built by artist Dionicio Rodriguez (who claimed to be a descendant of the Aztec race of Mexico) in the 1930's. There are traditional religious scenes, and some weird abstractions that perhaps only Aztecs understand. Look out folks, there's one opening near you soon.

# MAMMOTH CAVE
## Mammoth Cave National Park, Kentucky

What you can say about Mammoth Cave would fit into a large book, so a mere single page does it no justice at all. In Mammoth's enormous subterranean world there are sights that will astound you, and at 350 miles long and 379ft deep Kentucky's Mammoth Cave is easily the longest cave in the world, dwarfing its nearest challenger (Ukranian cave Optimisticeskaya) which is only a quarter of Mammoth's length. In fact exploration continues to this day in Mammoth Cave with more surprises being discovered every year.

Mammoth Cave National Park is simply gigantic offering over 53,000 acres of scenic parkland where hiking, fishing and wildlife viewing are all popular pursuits. It was established in 1941 to preserve the multitude of cavernous domes, underground rivers and lakes, unusual animals and plants, and the labyrinth of passages and tunnels that comprise Mammoth Cave. The park itself has a 300 acre, old-growth forest and is home to more than 200 species of birds, such is its size.

Underground rivers such as the River Styx and Echo River flow through the deepest of Mammoth Cave's chambers, and the quiet, dark passageways may seem to be devoid of life but in reality conceal a quite startling variety of animal life. Biologists have discovered over 200 species of animal in Mammoth Cave including 42 types of troglobites, which are animals exclusively adapted to life in complete darkness. The diversity is unrivalled anywhere in the world. The many rare and unusual animals who live here include ghostly white spiders, eyeless fish, and blind beetles. Numerous others are trogloxenes (cave visitors) who regularly visit or hibernate in the caves. There are 12 species of bats including 2 endangered species that live here, although not in large numbers. One of the most common species in Mammoth Cave, the little Brown Bat, can eat 600-700 mosquitoes in an hour. You will also see a lot of crickets here who spend much of their life in the cave but at night-time go to the surface in search of food. Crickets, which are a kind of grasshopper, play an important role in the cave as the bat population is not huge. They provide energy for other animals in the cave by way of eggs, droppings and carcasses. Another group of cave animals, the troglophiles (cave lovers), can survive their entire lives in caves but can also live permanently on the surface where they seek out cool, dark places. This group includes salamanders, crayfish and spiders, all found in Mammoth Cave.

Sparkling white gypsum crystals adorn some of the passages and shafts at Mammoth Cave whilst the magnificent sculpted shapes of some of the cave formations are breathtaking. The darkness and silence is all around and the cave has its own rhythms and cycles of life. The cave is very much different from our own world but for the survival of the vast complexity of cave life that lives within to continue, it is very much dependant on the outside world. Plants provide food and energy for the animals that live underground, and through photosynthesis and decay release carbon dioxide that combines with water in the soil and air to form a weak carbonic acid that carves the cave. Mammoth Cave is simply quite breathtaking and must be seen.

# LURAY CAVERNS
**970 US Highway 211,
West Luray, Virginia**

Luray Caverns is home to the world's only stalacpipe organ (seen opposite page) which creates music of concert quality from the surrounding stalactite formations that cover more than 3 acres. These beautiful yet haunting tones are the result of efforts by a certain Mr Leland Sprinkle (what an unusual name) who, in 1954, searched the vast caverns for stalactites that would create perfect sound. He wired the stalactites with rubber-tipped mallets and connected the individual wires to the organ meaning today's

visitors can listen to something quite unique.

A US Natural Landmark, Luray Caverns has cathedral sized rooms with the ceilings up to 10 storeys high. Huge towering stone columns, a fantastic variety of formations, and crystal clear pools all make Luray Caverns what it is today - Eastern America's biggest and most popular caverns.

# CASCADE CAVERNS
**226 Cascade Caverns Road,
Boerne, Texas**

These caverns are probably named after the cascading 100ft waterfall (see opposite page) that shoots over the rock-face of the last chamber with public access here. The usual cave formations can be seen, and the usual cave propaganda is shot at you; once voted best showcave, only Texas showcave with waterfall, etc, but it is the early folklore and history of the caverns that is the most interesting aspect of them.

First identified as being used by primitive people, they were subsequently occupied by Indians - who undoubtably practised Indian rituals here. Allegedly, it was only discovered by modern man when a cow fell down a sink-hole! During the 19th century a hermit who was a German immigrant lived here in a small cave where some steps lead down to. He lived here for the rest of his life, died when he was 45, and his bones were subsequently discovered long after.

Some of the formations at Cascade Caverns are quite unusual such as the Giant Molar, the naming of which does not need explanation. An abundance of pale cave crickets live in the caverns.

*The world's only stalacpipe organ (above) can be seen and heard at Luray Caverns, eastern America's largest caverns.*
*Cascade Caverns showcave in Texas has a 100ft waterfall (right) that cascades down a rock face. The Caverns have a constant 68F climate which is a welcome respite from the often unbearable Texas heat.*

# INNER SPACE CAVERN
## Georgetown, Texas

During the spring of 1963 a Texas Highway Department drilling team was taking samples to ascertain if the ground was stable enough to support a highway overpass. As one of the test holes was being drilled the drill bit suddenly dropped off and plunged some 20-30ft through the hole it had created. Further test drills in the area confirmed that a gigantic cavity was underneath and the workmen broke through into what is now known as Inner Space Cavern. The intrepid workman that was lowered into the void was probably the first human being to enter this stunning place. This natural cavern formed millions of years ago has spectacular rock formations and beautiful displays of helectites, sodastraws, cave drapery, and much more.

Unusually, you descend into the cavern on a unique cable-car system. The comfortable year-round temperature of 72 degrees makes the visit very pleasant and a paved walkway leads you through many rooms that have vivid and unusual formations. The 'Flowing Stone of Time' and 'Lake of the Moon' are some of the fantastic sights that await you amongst the many spectacular displays.

Several animals from the Ice Age have been discovered at Inner Space Cavern including bones from mammoths and sabre-toothed tigers. Albino crickets can be seen here, although they were everyday black crickets before venturing into the cavern and having to live without light. They slowly lose their colour and their antennas grow to 4 times the normal length to assist 'feeling' in the dark.

# SHENANDOAH CAVERNS
## 261 Caverns Road, Virginia

Virginia has many natural wonders and Shenandoah Caverns is one of its very best. It was discovered in 1884 by a group of boys who were amazed at the size and sheer beauty of the place. A crevice had been caused by a blast during construction of the Valley Division of the Southern Railway. This aroused the curiosity of a group of boys who descended through the crevice on a rope to a depth of 150ft. The light of their candles revealed a magnificent cavern, but it was not to be until 1921 that the caverns were fully developed, subsequently opening to the public in 1922.

Sights at Shenandoah Caverns, and thrilling sights they are, include the sparkling Diamond Cascade, the massive Grotto of the Gods, and the colourful Rainbow Lake. Cave formations here are so unusual they have been featured in National Geographic magazine and, incidentally, this is one of very few caverns that has elevator service!

There are 17 soaring rooms to be viewed at the caverns where thousands of stalactite and stalagmite formations can be seen. Unique 'bacon' formations, beautiful flowstone, and superb colouring as a result of water moving through limestone are all quite striking. The colouring of the caverns comes from pigments of magnesium, iron, and other minerals which water seeps through, although the limestone deposits are pure white.

# Part Three
## - REST OF WORLD -

*Akiyoshi-do is said to be the largest and most splendid cave in Asia. The 'Goddess of Mercy' seen above, and over 500 terraced limestone pools are some of the sights to be seen - page 71.*

## HALL OF BONES - BEINHAUS
### Hallstatt, Austria

'Hall' is said to be an old Celtic word for 'salt', and 'statt' means 'town'. Hallstatt is an old salt-mining hillside village where it is still possible to visit the ancient mines. The town also has 2 churches and in the predominantly Roman Catholic Austria, Hallstatt is one of very few places in Europe to have a 'Charnel House'. Visitors to this quiet, nondescript town will be shocked to see what lies within.

*Charnel House at Hallstatt.*

Before cremation was an acceptable way of disposing of the dead, the tiny graveyard of Hallstatt's Catholic church held buried persons for only a limited amount of time - usually about 8 - 12 years per body. After this they were exhumed to make way for the more recently dead. The church's Charnel

House ('beinhaus' or 'bone-house') has thousands of those bones and skulls that were exhumed now on display, with almost all of the sun-bleached skulls identified by the names, dates, or decorative markings that were put upon them by relatives when they were dug up. When cremation was approved by the Catholic Church in the 1960's this practice of exhumation ceased

*Named and decorated skulls at the Hall of Bones.*

## FONTANELLE CEMETERY
### Naples, Italy

Another charnel house, or ossuary as they are sometimes called, is located at the Fontanelle Cemetery in a cave on the hillside of the Materdei region of the city. Originally used to inter the dead during the early 1500's, the caves were subsequently in use as a mass burial ground from 1656 to address the severe burial problem caused by the plague. Thousands of anonymous corpses who

*Sombre sights as you witness the resting place of thousands of poor, anonymous souls. This is Fontanelle Cemetery.*

were victims of the great plague joined those already in this macabre place as with approximately 1,500 deaths a day from the plague, there was simply no space to put the bodies anywhere else. At that time graves were even being dug in streets.

It is believed that sometime in the late 1600's great floods washed out many of the remains in the caves on to the streets, which was a quite harrowing sight. The remains were returned to the cave and were to be joined by thousands more during the cholera epidemic of 1837.

In 1872 Father Gaetano Barbati had the horrific mounds of tangled skeletal remains disinterred and catalogued. They were stored in boxes, makeshift crypts, and even on wooden racks. A cult seems to have developed in Naples from this time which has subsequently been referred to as the 'cult of devotion to the skulls'. This lasted into the mid-20th century and saw devotees 'adopting' skulls whereby they would clean and polish them, offer prayers and light candles for them, bring flowers, and even give names to many. Many believed that this would speed their passage from purgatory to paradise. A small church was even built at the entrance.

In 1969, Cardinal Ursi of Naples decided that the cult had developed into a fashion of fetishism and Fontanelle

Cemetery was closed. At the time, defenders of the cult sprang to their defence pointing out that they were only giving some respect to those who had received none in either life or death, and had not been afforded the opportunity of even a decent burial. This curious relationship between Neapolitans and death is still evident today as the cemetery has since undergone restoration and can be visited once again. Visitors gasp in awe at the vast piles of bones of the nameless dead. Shinbones, thighbones, and a multitude of bleached skulls are all neatly stacked in a variety of shapes and ways. Many people still offer psalms and prayers to the poor souls whose unmarked remains lie on grisly show, exhibited to all who care to enter this foreboding place.

# DRAGON PALACE
**Longtan, near Anshun City,
Guizhou Province, China**

This very scenic area is a veritable wonderland of limestone caves, waterfalls, and underground waterways. At 9 miles in length the Dragon Palace is the prime attraction, and unlike other mountain caves in China, it is actually a group of 5 continous water eroded caverns linked by a long underground stream. They can all be seen by taking one of the boat trip tours.

In front of the Dragon Palace is an alpine lake surrounded by huge cliffs and rocks. This is called the Heavenly Lake and is the source of the quite stunning 40 metre high underground waterfall in front of the Palace Cave. One of the 5 caves (Crystal Palace) is steeped in legend and It is said that the Dragon King lives here.

Your boat trip through each of the caves takes you along 5,000 metres of underground river where you will be enthralled by a landscape which is completely illuminated in wonderful colours. No words can adequately describe these festive looking scenes. At some points the cave top soars 80 metres above whilst at others it is only a few metres high and wide.

# ELEPHANTA CAVES
**Elephanta Island,
near Mumbai, India**

In ancient times Elephanta Island was known as 'Gharapuri' or 'The Place of the Caves'. When the Portuguese took possession of the island they named it Elephanta after the huge statue they found on the seashore. Hewn out of solid rock, the Elephanta Caves can be dated back to 600AD and they consist of 7 caves, the most important of which is the Mahesha-Murti Cave. The whole of the cave complex is a vast collection of courtyards, grand halls and shrines, and is said to resonate with the spiritual energy of India.

The cave temple, dedicated to Lord Shiva, was excavated as far back as the 8th century by the Rashtrakuta Kings who ruled the area between 757AD and 973AD. There are some quite remarkable images within the sculptured compartments of this cave including those of Andhakari-Murti slaying an Andhaka demon, and Ravana shaking Kailasha. In fact throughout the entire area of the chambers and corridors of these magnificent rock cut temples, there are exquisite stone sculptures of Hindu Gods and Goddesses to be seen. Representations from Indian mythology can be seen carved on many walls, and enigmatic images are everywhere.

Shiva is portrayed and depicted here in many guises including 8 manifest forms. The Sadasiva manifestation of Shiva is a sight to behold. Carved in relief at the end of the north-south axis, this immense 20ft high image of the 3-headed Shiva, each head depicting a different form, is quite stunning and is considered to be a masterpiece of Indian art.

Legends can be seen portrayed everywhere throughout this amazing 60,000 sq.ft cave complex perfectly expressed in sculptures, beautiful reliefs, and the temples dedicated to Lord Shiva. No visit to India would be complete without a worthwhile journey to the Elephanta Caves.

# ITHAA UNDERSEA RESTAURANT
## Hilton Maldives Resort & Spa, Rangali Island, Maldives

The Maldives is a nation of coral islands that is scattered across the Indian Ocean. It gained independence in 1965 and a more beautiful setting could not be imagined for the first ever all-glass undersea restaurant in the world. It was created by MJ Murphy Ltd, a design consultancy based in New Zealand, and its distinctive feature is the curved acrylic walls and roof which are 125mm thick. There are 5 of these acrylic arches which are sealed to each other and the structure with a special silicone sealant, and the structure itself was built in Singapore before being shipped to the Island on a massive barge; the barge being equipped with a giant crane to lower it into position in the sea. Incredibly, the structure weighed 175 tons, and a further 85 tons of sand was added to the belly of the structure to sink it into the sea. The project cost $5 million to complete which means an astronomical amount of dishes have to be served up to recoup investment costs.

Seating 14 patrons comfortably, the experience of dining in Ithaa's translucent shell is akin to being in a giant aquarium. Submerged 16ft below sea level the restaurant offers panoramic underwater views, providing diners with a face-to-face experience of the stunning beauty of the Indian Ocean. While you are eating your starters a myriad of startingly coloured fish swim by with their eyes diverted in the direction of you. Your main course may be accompanied by an unexpected guest or 2 as giant rays hover above, their bodies generating wave-like movements in the crystal clear clarity of the surrounding sea. The sweet course should be enjoyed to the full - if nothing else but to prepare you for the bill you are about to be presented with.

It has to be said that although expensive the 'fusion cuisine' (western food items with Maldivian elements) is on a par with what you would find at top London restaurants, with the added bonus of these beautiful surroundings.

A coral garden has been planted on the nearby reef encouraging many more colourful fish to live there. This enhances the spectacular views that diners have of not just the fish, but also sharks, rays, and many more aquatic creatures who are attracted here.

Yungang Grottoes (above) which have an astonishing 51,000 statues of Buddhist carvings, and (below right) one of the larger statues which is well over 10 metres high. The walkway leading into Akiyoshi-do Cave (bottom left) which plunges to 100 metres below ground.

## YUNGANG GROTTOES
### Datong, Shanxi Province, China

Yungang Grottoes can be found at the foot of Wuzhou Mountain approximately 16km from Datong City. It is an extraordinary complex of 45 grottoes carved into the cliffs and contains an astounding 51,000 stone Buddhist carvings, the largest of which is 17 metres high. This treasure trove of Buddhist art is one of China's most famous places and is unrivalled anywhere in the world today.

Yungang Grottoes consist of over 52 caves which are home to the 45 grottoes. Most of them were carved between 460 and 494AD under the instructions of a Buddhist monk named Tan Yao during the Northern Wei Dynasty. They may have been inspired by the caves at Dunhuang (Mogao Grottoes) which were started over 100 years earlier, are hewn from solid rock, and represent some of the oldest in China.

The caves at Yungang stretch about 1km from east to west and the earliest work certainly has western origins. This is evident by the lions, Persian and Byzantine weapons, and Greek tridents. There are also images of Hindu gods Shiva and Vishnu, and representations of Chinese culture in the form of dragons, flying asparas, etc. This huge range and diversity of subject matter is a combination of Chinese and foreign artistic beauty. The majority of the carvings are precise in detail and exquisite to behold; the result of ceaseless devotion by the skilled stone-carvers and other craftsmen who worked upon them.

Although the majority of the caves are closed to the public some of the most stunning are not. Within these the visitor can admire beauty as well as magnitude; the largest Buddha statue being enshrined in the middle of Cave Number 5 is 17 metres high, and either side of the entrance to the cave is a Buddha statue in sitting posture under the bodhi tree.

## AKIYOSHI-DO CAVE
### Syuuhou-tyo, Yamaguchi, Japan

Although visited by English schoolmaster George Edward Gauntlett in 1907, it was not until 1926 - following a visit by the Showa Emperor when he was still the Crown Prince - that the cave received its name in his honour.

Akiyoshi-do Cave is the largest calcareous cave in Japan and is found approximately 100 metres below ground. The natural entrance to the cave is at the foot of a 150ft high cliff and is entered via a specially constructed walkway (see picture opposite). At 20 metres high and 8 metres wide this is one of the most dramatic entrances of any cave in Asia, particularly in view of the fact that an underground stream is gushing out. The tourist route runs parallel to this stream for most of the journey. Said to be the largest cave in Asia, visitors will see large columns and stalagmites, and a complex of over 500 terraced limestone pools which are unusual and quite unique.

## DEER CAVE
**Gunung Mulu National Park, Sarawak, Mulu, Malaysia**

Deer Cave is a through-cave with 2 enormous entrances and an unusual rock formation at one opening that strangely resembles Abraham Lincoln's profile. The other opening is commonly known as the Garden of Eden because of the lush jungle that surrounds it. At over 100 metres wide and 120 metres high, one entrance is said to be the highest cave entrance in the world.

This unusual cave has a phenomenal population of bats - in particular Wrinkle-lipped Bats of which there are about 5 million. Shortly before dusk when great hordes of these creatures leave the cave is like a scene from a Hammer Horror film and this great colony, said to be the world's largest bat colony, can eat about 10 tons of insects in a single night. It truly is one of nature's greatest spectacles.

## JAMEOS DEL AGUA
**Lanzarote, Canarias, Spain**

Attractions at this unusual resort include a series of caverns and smaller caves used in a variety of ways. One of the largest caverns has superb acoustics and is used as a concert hall, whilst others have been turned into trendy bars and restaurant.
Vulcanology played an important role in the creation of this area and the caves formed as lava tubes. An on-site museum on the subject explains more. There is also a beautiful subterranean lagoon which is always popular with tourists and contains a diversity of rare animal species.

## BARTON CREEK CAVE
**Upper Barton Creek Village, San Ignacio, Belize**

This huge cave was believed by the Maya to be the Underworld, or 'Xibalba', the Kingdom of the Gods. There are ancient Maya ruins scattered throughout Belize and a pristine rainforest is here for all to enjoy. The Maya were a race riddled with superstitions and beliefs and they carried out many sacrifices here in Barton Creek Cave. Your boat journey through this mystical subterranean landscape takes you past many old skeletons and other remains, including one that is said to be that of a virgin who was sacrificed to attract a rain god.

The cave itself has a large bat population and fantastic speleothems that are millions of years old.

*Where exactly is Belize? Most people assume in South America but it is in fact in the heart of Central America. This unspoilt Caribbean playground lies just below Mexico near Guatemala, next to the Western Caribbean Sea, and is really not that far from the United States.*

*Britain ruled this land for almost 2 centuries and until 1973 it was known as British Honduras. It became independent in 1981.*

*The total area of Belize is 8,867 square miles.*

# NUREMBERG ART BUNKER
## Obere Schmiedgasse 52, Nuremberg, Germany

There was first evidence of cellars here as far back as 1380 and it is known that they were also in use as medieval wine cellars, but their most important use was not finalised until 1938 when secret meetings were held to create plans for an art bunker.

There were 3 high ranking city government officials of Nuremberg who did not believe in 'Blitzkrieg' or 'Endsieg'. Dr. Konrad Fries, Heinz Schmeibner, and Julius Linke made preparation - in case of a possible war - to save important masterpieces of art. They planned to use the medieval rock-cut cellars which were 24 metres beneath the castle hill to store them, and planned all the details for conversion and climate control. When the war ultimately started they began work the very day after and in just 6 months it was complete. The whole operation was illegal and would have meant the concentration camp for all 3 if they were discovered. Money was siphoned off from the works departments of the 3 initiators to cover materials and costs.

Although the cellar rooms were damp and cold the walls were given a lining of clinker, then walls and ceilings were painted with waterproof tar. The next layer was fibreglass for thermal insulation, then Heraklit boards (made of wood and cement), and finally a cardboard panelling. The heating system used was 2 big coal ovens and 2 air conditioning systems, allowed to cool to condense water and regulate humidity. Upon completion of the bunker the storage of art started. The Mayor of Nuremberg, many priests, and those in charge of valuable objects all started to discreetly and secretly transfer important works. Even the Chief of Nuremberg Police co-operated. When the official order from the Nazi's came to save all valuable objects, the majority of them were already in the bunker. During the war this is said to have been the highest concentration of important art treasures in Europe. Whilst the devastating bombing attacks of the Second World War levelled most of old Nuremberg, most of its artistic treasures and heritage survived.

Today, the original installations can still be seen at the bunker but its treasures are long gone, most returned whence they came. Not a single piece was damaged or lost due to the foresight and courage of 3 Nuremberg citizens and their meticulous planning.

*Trance-like devotees (above) celebrating the Hindu Festival of Thaipusam at Batu Caves use skewers and hooks to pierce their skin, but apparently feel no pain, and (below) the 272 steps which must be climbed to reach the impressive entrance to Batu Caves.*

# BATU CAVES
## Kuala Lumpur, Malaysia

Batu Caves are one of Malaysia's great natural wonders consisting of 3 main caves and numerous smaller ones. The Temple Cave (or Cathedral Cave as it is better known) is a massive chamber lit by daylight from several gaps or holes in the ceiling. It is called the Temple Cave as it contains several shrines, and the Sri Subramania Swamy Temple which is a focal point for the renowned Hindu Festival of Thaipusam each year.

Below the Temple Cave is the Dark Cave which can only be entered with permission from the Malaysian Nature Society. This is a 2km network of caverns containing a lage number of endemic cave animals including several species found nowhere else in the world. At the foot of the steps to the Dark Cave is the Gallery Cave containing, as the name would imply, an art gallery that has statues and wall paintings depicting scenes from Hindu mythology.

To reach the entrance to Batu Caves you have to climb 272 rock steps, which can prove strenuous in the heat and with macaque monkeys vying for your attention; but this is exactly what over a million devotees do every January to celebrate the spectacular, if somewhat unusual, Festival of Thaipusam. This is a colourful celebration of Lord Subramaniam, a Hindu deity of youth, power and virtue, and is not for the squeamish. It commemorates the day on which the Goddess Parvathi gave her son Murugan an invincible vel (lance) with which he vanquished the evil asura (demons). It may seem strange and bizarre to outsiders who see grown people piercing steel hooks into their chest, back and face, but this is one of the ways in which many penitents express their devotion.

The festival starts with a procession through the town and a silver chariot carries the image of Lord Subramaniam. People throw coconuts on the ground towards it as it passes. En masse, the devotees then head for the pilgrimage site of Batu Caves. Penitents atone for their sins and commemorate the giving of the 'vel' by bearing or carrying 'kavadis' (burdens) up the 272 steps before leaving them at the feet of the deity. This is one of the most incredible sights you are ever likely to witness as a sea of a million people, some praying and some in a trance-like state, make their way towards the caves. Many of them carry these kavadis which are various metal frames that can weigh up to 50lbs. They are attached to the bearer with various metal hooks and skewers that are inserted into the skin of the chest, back, and frequently the arms and face. Others carry paal kudam (a pot laden with milk) to 'bathe' the deities with the milk. The more devoted (or is it flamboyant and brave) followers put skewers through their tongues and cheeks to represent the 'vel', whilst the odd person can be spotted with just a few dozen steel hooks protuding from their backs. It is said that because they are in trance they cannot feel any pain, and surely a million people can't be wrong. There was one guy who was shouting and chanting louder than at a football match, but he never got arrested. They let him off the hook.

# CAPUCHIN CATACOMBS
## Palermo, Sicily, Italy

There are numerous places to view mummified bodies if you are so inclined but the Capuchin Catacombs are without doubt the most gruesome place in the world to see them. Located in the city of Palermo on the Italian island of Sicily, this is frequently referred to as the 'Museum of Death' - and not without good reason as there are over 8,000 mummies dating back to the 16th century lining the walls of the catacombs here. Eerie, sombre and

intriguing, the most bizarre aspect of it all is that they give off no smell whatsoever. The assembled ranks of the dead, many with quite elegant costumes that have decayed over the years, are mainly skeletons - although some still have mummified flesh, hair, and even eyes. Others have spectacles on and a good percentage have quite horrific expressions on their distorted faces. Many appear to be screaming in death as time and gravity have distorted the corpses, and some have body parts which have fallen off such as feet, hands, parts of the skull and jaws, etc.

During the 16th century when the Capuchin monks of Palermo removed some bodies from their graves they discovered that they had undergone a natural mummification. With the religious aspect in mind, local priests mummified the body of a holy monk (Brother Silvestro) for public viewing. Many local families wanted the same treatment for their deceased relatives and the catacombs rapidly filled up. It would appear that this mummification treatment became something of a status symbol as many people specified in their wills which clothes they wanted to be dressed in when dead. Others even asked for a change of garments a certain time after their death, and monks were interred in religious robes complete with items of penance around their necks.

The process of mummification was done by laying the bodies in rooms in the catacombs to undergo dehydration. Following this the bodies were washed in vinegar and some were embalmed to help preserve appearance. Others were enclosed in sealed glass. Once the mummies had been fully prepared they were clothed and placed on the walls. A law passed by the Italian government

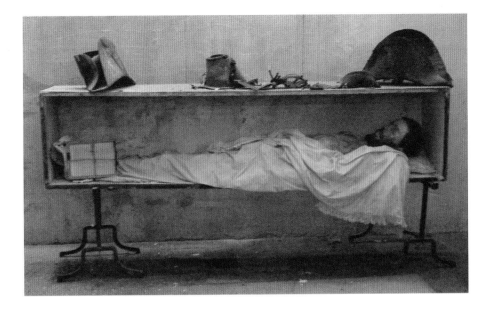

in 1881 meant the catacombs were no longer allowed to continue with this mummification process, although special permission from the government saw the interring of a 2 year old child called Rosalia Lombardo in 1920. She is known as the 'Sleeping Beauty' and it is said that her sister and other members of her family often visited her after her death. Her body is still perfectly intact to this day and she can be seen propped up in a glass case. The method for embalming her was invented by Dr.Solafia, a Palermo doctor, but the secret of his expertise was taken to his grave. Children interred here are often posed and there are even 2 of them seated together in a rocking chair.

The halls of the catacombs are divided into categories and social stratification is respected here. There are sections for men, women, children, priests, monks, professionals, and even virgins. The professors section contains the bodies of professors, doctors, painters, lawyers, and officers and soldiers of the Bourbon and Italian army. Some of the most famous names here are the painter Velasquez, and sculptor Lorenzo Marabitti.

One wall of the catacombs is completely devoted to women's corpses, apparent by the presence of skirts, dresses and parasols. Many bodies throughout the catacombs can be seen lying down or in seated posture, in addition to the thousands of corpses that line the walls like paintings. Included here are hundreds of coffins as well, with many containing the corpse that was buried in them. The side is often cut to expose the deceased which makes a tour of the Capuchin Catacombs all the more scary as you never know what is lurking around the next corner.

Perhaps today's relatives of the deceased who lie (or stand) in perpetual limbo are happy for their ancestors to be a spectacle for the numerous tourists that Capuchin Catacombs attracts each year. I wonder. Surely its a case of the dead working for the living by providing tourism revenue for the city.

## CHRISTIAN CATACOMBS OF ROME
**Rome, Italy**

In the first century Rome's Christians did not have their own cemeteries. Only common cemeteries where pagans were buried existed, so anyone owning their own land would obviously bury relatives there instead. During the early second century grants enabled the catacombs to be founded and Christians started burying their dead underground. The catacombs are made up of underground tunnels in the form of a vast labyrinth, and because Christians preferred underground burials (as Christ was buried) instead of cremation, the development of the catacombs rapidly grew. Digging underground tunnels and galleries was also much less inexpensive than buying large tracts of land for cemeteries. In compliance with Roman law which did not permit burial of the dead within the city walls, all catacombs are located outside the city, many along the consular roads.

There are more than 60 catacombs in Rome although only a handful are open to the public. They represent hundreds of miles of galleries and maybe 40,000 tombs, and are visited today by tens of thousands of pilgrims from all over the world because of their importance. The resting place of saints and martyrs, and a depository of paintings and sculptures, etc; every inscription in every gallery of the vast complex of the catacombs gives a message of faith and Christian belief, speaking as much of life as death.

The enormous scale of the catacombs is truly immense with a multi-levelled network of galleries. The burials of early Christians were very simple and the corpses - wrapped in a shroud in imitation of Christ - were placed in the 'loculi' (a cut out niche) then closed with a slab of marble or tiles and mortar. Sometimes the name of the deceased was added, or a Christian symbol. Besides the loculi there were other forms of tombs in the catacombs such as the arcosolium ( a larger niche with an arch that was big enough for an entire family), sarcophagus, cubicula (small rooms), and crypts which were were akin to small underground churches adorned with decorations.

A guild of workers known as 'fossores' worked on the catacombs, digging gallery after gallery by faint lights. Air-vents for light as well as ventilation were added, and thousands worked tirelessly on this project of mammoth proportions.

## THE CATACOMBS OF PARIS
**Paris, France**

Most of the Catacombs of Paris can be found at the base of 3 mountains; Montparnasse, Montsouris, and Montrouge. There are approximately 300km of galleries in the catacombs, and the small part that is open to the public is certain to shock, and is not for those of a nervous disposition.

Overcrowding in medieval cemeteries in the centre of Paris at the end of the 18th century led to the government creating subterranean mass graves. Over the course of 18 months, from 1785, the bones and rotting corpses of 6 million people were moved in large carts across the city at night to a new resting place. Here they are arranged in huge piles at the 'Empire of Death'.

*An alleyway to the dead (above left) at the Christian Catacombs of Rome, ancient underground cemeteries built by 'fossores' (gravediggers). The Catacombs of Paris (top right and below) has sometimes been referred to as 'The Empire of Death'. This network of about 200 miles of underground galleries contains millions of bones. Although only a single mile of this vast place is open to the public, visitors will see thousands of bones in one room - and there are dozens of rooms to visit. The human bones, including countless skulls, are arranged in many configurations such as crosses, faces, wall ornamentation, or simply huge mounds. A strong stomach needed here.*

*The entrance for a boat trip through the spectacular Waitomo Glow-worm Caves (above) and (below), millions of minute Arachnocampa Luminosa (glow-worms) light up the Caves. They hang their feeding lines from horizontal ceilings.*

# WAITOMO GLOW-WORM CAVES
## Waitomo, Otorohanga, New Zealand

A journey unlike no other you will ever experience is a subterranean boat trip into the spectacular Glow-worm Grotto of Waitomo Glow-worm Caves in New Zealand. The feeling of awe as you glide silently through the Grotto, beneath a starry wonderland lit up by the activities of millions of tiny glow-worms, is something you will remember throughout your life.

The Waitomo network of limestone caves attracts up to a million visitors a year and their guided tour takes you through over 250 metres of stunning underground scenery. The acoustics in the Cathedral Cavern are world renowned, whilst other impressive cave formations include the Pipe Organ, Catacombs, and Tomo, which is a deep limestone shaft.

The Glow-worm Grotto (as it is known) is spectacularly illuminated by a phenomenon known as 'bioluminescence' which is produced by the females to attract males whilst in the final stage of their pupal development. Without this magnificent display the cave would be pitch-black. The feeling you get as you silently float beneath this sea of minute lights is that of being under a star filled sky. It is only the sound of dripping water that reminds you that you are in a deep underground cave. This cave has been known to the Maori population for centuries but it was only in the late 19th century that it was discovered by Europeans, and subsequently opened to the public in 1911.

*Arachnocampa luminosa (glow-worms) are 2 winged insects no bigger than a mosquito. They are a somewhat rare phenomenon as the perfect conditions for their safe reproduction - darkness, humidity, very little wind, and a reasonable food supply - are rarely met in full.*

*The whole lifecycle of a glow-worm takes just under a year. Eggs are laid in clutches on walls and ceilings and the instant they are hatched the larvae emits a light. They then build a nest and put down lines for feeding. Sticky substances on the lines trap small insects which are hauled up to be eaten. They feed only in the larvae stage and store sufficient food to survive the pupa and adult stages.*

*Shortly before the pupa stage the light of the female becomes more brilliant to attract the male, and at the emergence from the pupa stage they shrink, become opaque, then rest, mate, and restart the cycle.*

*The female fly lays just over a hundred eggs which hatch in around 20 days. They are less than 2mm long each but soon grow, and even at this tiny size they emit a good visible light. The instinct is to crawl upward until they reach a horizontal ceiling to hang their feeding lines, but they are often eaten by spiders or older glow-worms on the way.*

*The adult glow-worm has no mouth and its only function is to reproduce. Frequently, a male is waiting for the female to emerge from the pupa and mating takes place instantly. If a male is not waiting she flies to nearby colonies of glow-worms and emits a strong light. The flies last no longer than a few days and may be eaten by other insects.*

## MILK GROTTO CHAPEL
### Bethlehem, Israel

The legends surrounding the Milk Grotto Chapel are many and varied and this is the place where, according to Christian tradition, the Holy Family took shelter during the Slaughter of the Innocents by Herod's soldiers. It is said that whilst Mary was breast-feeding the baby Jesus some of the milk was spilt onto the floor. This is supposed to have made the rock crumble and, as this was the milk that fed the Son of God, a remarkable pilgrimage cult has grown alongside the legend.

   Mothers - both Christian and Muslim - journey here to buy packets of the powdered white stone of the grotto which is said to increase the quality and amount of milk created by lactating mothers, by putting the powdery white stone into drinking water. As the white chalky rock resembles the colour of milk this seems reasonable, but in reality any benefits gained should be attributed to the calcium in the rock. Others take the rock home to place under their bed, but wouldn't it be easier, and cheaper, to simply order a few extra pints from your milkman?

## GROTTO OF GETHSEMANE
### Jerusalem, Israel

Mentioned as far back as 1333 by German Dominican Wilhelm von Boldensele, the Grotto of Gethsemane is the place where Jesus, having been betrayed by Judas, was arrested. The grotto is located in a cave which has 3 altars together with paintings of the Assumption of the Virgin, the Kiss of Judas, and Jesus praying amongst the Apostles. Of all the holy places in Israel this would appear to be conserved nearest to how its original appearance may have looked over 2,000 years ago. Also called the Grotto of the Agony as it was thought to be the precise location of the Agony of Jesus, tens of thousands of visitors pay homage at this holy location each year.

## GROTTO OF THE NATIVITY
### Bethlehem, Israel

The Grotto of the Nativity is another holy place revered in Christianity. Beneath it is the Altar of the Nativity which is said to be the exact spot where Jesus was born. This is marked by a hole in the marble flow beneath the altar.

## CAVE CHURCH - GROTTO OF ST.PETER IN ANTIOCH
### Antioch-on-the Orontes, Antakya, Turkey

This is believed to mark the location of the meetings of the first church community in Antioch which was founded by the apostles Peter and Paul. Dating back to the 2nd century BC, St.Peter preached and founded the Christian community here and it was declared as a Holy Place by the Vatican in 1983. This cave church is said to be the first church built by man.

## WOLF'S LAIR
### Wilczy Szaniec, Gierloz, Poland

Hitler's headquarters at Gierloz was known as the Wolf's Lair and it is a grim reminder of the many thousands of Nazi slave workers who died whilst constructing these bunkers. The fortress is composed of 80 or so buildings, 50 of them being bunkers with 6 metre thick walls, and it was here that Adolf Hitler had his main headquarters between September 1941 and September 1944. Most of his time was spent here except for brief visits to Berchtesgaden and Berlin.

This is truly an enormous complex built under the supervision of the dreaded Todt Organization who were well known for ill treatment of prisoners. The

fortress had its own electric power generator, air-strip and railway station, and top Nazi officials had their own quarters and even a cinema and casino. The whole area would have been camouflaged and protected with minefields.

Fuhrer Bunker No.13 was Hitler's personal quarters and close by is a plaque that marks the spot where he was nearly assassinated on July 20th, 1944 by Colonel Claus von Staffenberg. It was unveiled by the sons of Staffenberg to commemorate their father and other participants of the failed assassination attempt who were murdered by the Nazi's. During the German retreat in January 1945 they attempted to blow up the fortress but their is still much of this bleak and sinister place to be seen today.

The Underground Catacomb Anglican Church (above left) is one of many subterranean wonders at the remarkable opal mining town of Coober Pedy in South Australia. There is even an underground pottery, museum, and art gallery, and approximately 80% of the population live underground as the temperature can rise to 60 degrees centigrade in summer. Because of opal mining, the town and surrounding area is riddled with tunnels. A sign (above right) warns of these perils in its own inimitable way.

This way in (left) to Beijing's Underground City and (below), one of the 40 or so subterranean settlements that comprise the Underground Cities of Cappadocia - once home to over 20,000 people. They descend 18 storeys into the Anatolian plateau with some dating back to 1200BC.

## MONTREAL UNDERGROUND CITY
**Montreal, Canada**

The largest underground complex in the world, Montreal's Underground City tunnels cover a remarkable 32km spread out over a total area of 12sq.km. Commercial and residential premises comprise a chunk of this, and in fact approximately 80% of all office space and 40% of all commercial space in downtown Montreal is located underground.

## COOBER PEDY
**Coober Pedy, South Australia**

Coober Pedy is one of the most unusual places in the world. It is a town where (due to the heat) approximately 80% of the population live and work underground. This is a mining town - opal mining to be precise - and following the early discovery of opals here by a teenager there has been a huge influx of miners since 1915. There are tunnels and associated pitfalls everywhere and mining still goes on here today.

There are many truly fascinating attractions around Coober Pedy, including underground homes to explore. Other subterranean structures operating in the same manner as an above ground equivalent include a church, shops, pottery, art gallery, hotel, and other assorted offices and businesses.

Some of the town's other must-see attractions include the Big Winch and the Oldtimers Mine, and the most unusual of all must surely be the golf course where not a single blade of grass can be seen. The fairways are bald and the greens are oiled sand!

## BEIJING UNDERGROUND CITY
**62 West Damochang Street, Qianmen, China**

Beijing's Underground City is actually an enormous network of bomb shelters beneath the capital. Some are officially open to tourists and many have been utilised for a variety of uses such as shopping centres, hostels and business operations. Over 1,000 of these old shelters are located between 10 and 20 metres below ground and could easily accommodate half the population of Beijing. They were built during the 1970's by an army of 300,000 men, women and children, and cover over 85sq.km consisting of 30km of passageways.

## UNDERGROUND CITIES OF CAPPADOCIA
**Cappadocia, Anatolia, Turkey**

There are 8 floors of labyrinthine tunnels open to visitors of the astonishing Underground Cities of Cappadocia. The sheer scale of them is mind-boggling and almost 40 of them have been discovered so far. They were originally constructed as temporary rather than permanent habitats and some of them date to approximately 1200BC. Not for the claustrophobic, these subterranean towns and cities were carved from soft volcanic stone, and large stone-rolling doors prevented invaders from entering. Deep wells and chimney vents; even livestock pens and churches were built underground enabling the inhabitants to live there for months at a stretch, or at least until it was safe to emerge.

## MARAKOOPA CAVES
**Mayberry, Mole Creek,
Tasmania, Australia**

Glow-worms are endemic to both
Australia and New Zealand, although
they are less common in Australia.
Marakoopa Caves however has an
abundance of them and they can be
seen - like a glorious stretch of the
night sky - on either of the 2 interesting
tours available. Marakoopa has 2 cave
rivers, admirable speleothems, and
huge caverns including the Great
Cathedral which is a quite magnificent
cavern. The Gardens is a cave branch
that boasts delicate formations in an
array of striking colours.

Tasmania, which promotes itself as
the 'Natural State', has a relatively
unspoiled natural environment. About
40% of it consists of National Parks,
reserves, and World Heritage Sites.

## WELLINGTON CAVES
**Wellington, New South Wales,
Australia**

Wellington Caves are actually dry caves
and they were formed when Australia
was a lot more southerly to the pole and
the climate much drier. The river
passages here are the only reminder of
a previous cave river, and visitors
today see only a floor covered with dry
earth. The caves were first explored by
Europeans from 1823-1831 when fossil
bones of a giant kangaroo, and those of
a diprotodon dating back to the
Pleistocene period were discovered.

Phosphate mining (operational here
from 1913 to 1971) is remembered with
the fully restored Phosphate Mine which
is now open to visitors.

Declared a natural reserve in 1884, by
far the most impressive cave here is the
Cathedral Cave. It is famous for a huge
stalagmite known as the Altar Rock
which is over 15 metres high and has a
base circumference of an astonishing
32 metres. The most important
discoveries at Wellington Caves have
been the River Cave and Water Cave,
both of which contain valuable fossils.

## NARACOORTE CAVES
**Naracoorte National Park,
South Australia**

Although this complex consists of 26
caves many are not open to the public
as they are set aside for important
scientific research, or to protect the
contents. There is so much to see at
Naracoorte Caves that visitors are truly
spoilt for choice. Several spectacular
chambers showcase some of the most
striking underground scenery you are
ever likely to see.

The Alexandra Cave Tour is one of
the many treasures here. This is a
beautifully decorated cave with a huge
collection of straws. The Victoria Fossil
Cave Tour passes through several
decorated chambers before arriving at
the Fossil Chamber itself. Fox Cave is
undeveloped and in its original state. It
is an important Bentwing bat wintering
location and also has many fossils and
a rare invertebrate colony. There is also
a dedicated Bat Tour which offers the
opportunity of observation platform
viewing via infra-red cameras.

The Starburst Chamber, Blackberry
Cave, Stick-Tomato Cave, and
Cathedral Cave are some of the many
other attractions in addition to speciality
tours. Naracoorte Caves National Park
has a host of other activities.

*Naracoorte Caves (above) in South Australia consists of 26 caves in total, whilst Marakoopa Caves (below) in Tasmania is known as the Handsome Cave, as 'marakoopa' is aboriginal for 'handsome'. This river cave also has the largest amount of glow-worms of any show cave in Australia.*

## MING TOMBS
### near Beijing City, Beijing, China

The Ming Tombs are the perfectly preserved mausoleums of 13 emperors of the Ming Dynasty (1368-1644). In the early 14th century the Yuan Dynasty (of Mongol stock) ruled China, but by 1356 it was in disarray and a number of swift campaigns - led by rebel leader Zhu Yuanzhang - ended with the overthrow of the Yuan Dynasty and the dawning of a new era led by the Ming, which in Chinese means 'bright'. Being of native Chinese origin the Ming created a powerful administration that eventually encompassed all the modern provinces, except Xinjiang.

Upon the death of Zhu Yuanzhang in 1398, power passed on to his grandson and successor, Zhu Jianwen, at the age of 21. A civil war erupted between the north and south and it was Zhu Di, an inspirational leader and general and also a direct descendant of Zhu Yuanzhang the Ming founder, who overthrew the reign of Zhu Jianwen. Zhu Di marched south and captured Nanjing, and then located a site in the northern plains where a workforce of a million labourers created a new capital (which would one day become Beijing) within 5 years.

Conscious of his own mortality he set about finding a burial site that would exemplify his status. About 40 kilometres north-west from Beijing a spot was selected in the shadow of a mountain called 'Heavenly Longevity', and it was here that Zhu Di and his 12 successors were buried in imperial splendour.

Only the Changling and Dingling tombs are open to the public. Changling, the chief of the Ming Tombs, is the largest and magnificently preserved. Dingling is 27 metres underground and is the mausoleum of Zhu Yigun, the 13th emperor, who together with his 2 empresses occupied the throne the longest during the Ming Dynasty. The Soul Tower, Baocheng, Stone Bridge, and Underground Palace (discovered in 1956) are its main features, and they are all quite astounding and many are very beautiful. Amongst the coffins is the gold imperial crown which is one of the world's most rare treasures.

The layout of each of the 13 mausoleums are similar, yet vary in size and complexity of structures. Changling is central, with the other 12 laid out around it. History, wonder and awe awaits the visitor here.

# CU CHI TUNNELS
## Cu Chi, near Ho Chi Minh City, Vietnam

The Cu Chi Tunnels, a 75 mile long underground maze where thousands of fighters and villagers could hide, are a remnant of the Vietnam War between the communist north and the western south and are a prime example of why the US army had very little success. The site of the old tunnels was once one of the most notorious battlegrounds of the Vietnam War and today is probably the country's best known tourist attraction.

The tunnels were built by hand to fit the small Vietcong guerillas. Originally they stretched all the way from Saigon to Ho Chi Minh Trail at the Cambodian border and were started during the war for independence from the French. Their construction continued for 25 years and many people lived in this underground city for years. The tunnels are truly impressive and this 3-level network includes kitchens, mess halls, meeting rooms, living quarters, schools, and even an operating theatre and small cinema, although their primary use was as communication and supply routes.

The construction of the tunnels was made possible because of the special geology of the area. Most of the region is covered with a thick layer of red clay which is the residual of tropical erosion and it is easy to manipulate and mine, whilst being strong enough not to collapse. Remarkably, it was dug out using only hand tools. Reed baskets were filled with the clay and the contents disposed of in a variety of ingenious places - quite often in bomb craters. The tunnels had vents for heating, fresh air, and of course to listen out for helicopters approaching.

It is known that the US Army built the headquarters of the 25th Infantry Division right over the top of part of the tunnels complex. After a lengthy period of time they discovered the tunnels but were unable to fully destroy them. American soldiers did not fit into the very narrow entrances or passages, and in any case they were riddled with deadly booby traps. Bombing them had little effect as the clay absorbed the shock waves, and any of the tunnels that were destroyed were immediately replaced anyway. The tunnels have been famously described as "the most bombed, shelled, gassed, defoliated, and generally devastated area in the history of warfare".

Today many of the tunnels are either filled in, destroyed, or in very poor condition, although quite a few of those intact are open to the public. These have been widened for easier access and have steps and lighting, but the claustrophobic feeling and surreal atmosphere is something that cannot be changed. Visitors to the tunnels are greeted by a sign that reads 'Please try to be a Cu Chi guerrilla. Wear these uniforms before entering tunnel'. The Vietnamese have turned the whole area into a money making machine and the woods are liberally dotted with kiosks selling items such as a lighter made from a bullet or the inevitable t-shirt that reads 'I've been to the Cu Chi Tunnels'. Soft drink stands, young women in the black pyjamas of the Vietcong strolling through the woods, and a guide around every corner usually dressed in fatigues are all common sights here. Shoot an AK-47 rifle or watch B-52's drop strings of bombs on widescreen television. All good fun for visitors but what about the 40,000 Vietnamese people who perished in the tunnels. A remembrance to them would make better use of the site. Good mourning Vietnam.

# DIEFENBUNKER
**3911 Carp Road, Carp,
near Ottowa, Ontario, Canada**

In 1959 Canada began the construction of a huge 4-storey bunker buried under a hillside, 35km from its capital city Ottawa. Over the next decade this was to be one of around 50 protective shelters put in place across the nation, but the facility at Carp was the 'flagship' as it would be resistant to the blast levels from 5 million tons of TNT exploding a mile away. The 'wind' passing over the structure from such a blast would have exceeded 1,000 miles per hour! Shelter in this Central Emergency Government Facility could accommodate approximately 535 people for about a month.

   The Diefenbunker, as it came to be known (after Prime Minister John Diefenbaker), has some amazing sights for visitors to see. Included amongst these are the mock-up of a basement, family fallout shelter, the Bank of Canada vault with a 2ft thick, 15 ton door, and a one megaton practice 'toss' bomb. This unique facility takes you into a virtual time warp to the 1960's era as you view government rooms, the War Cabinet Room, the CBC radio station, and living quarters. Over 100,000 sq.ft in size, Diefenbunker is a magnificent achievement and the tour, which lasts about an hour and a half, is a real eye-opener.

   Another part of the complex worth mentioning is the Blast Tunnel which would allow a blast wave to enter at one end and exit the other, without creating undue pressure on the main entrance. It is large enough to permit cars and trucks to pass through.

# FORTRESS FURIGEN
**Lake Lucerne, Kehrsiten,
Switzerland**

There were 20,000 bunkers dug into the sides of The Alps as peaceful Switzerland wanted to stay neutral during the hostilities of war. This elaborate system of bunkers and fortresses is quite remarkable and Bunker Furigen, one of few open to the public, must be seen. You enter through a plain looking wooden barrack, put on an original Swiss Army coat to keep out the cold, and find yourself in a world of Swiss secrecy. The museum here has an abundance of 20th century weaponry.

# VILLA TORLONIA - MUSSOLINI'S BUNKER
**Rome, Italy**

The park of Villa Torlonia is the most notable English landscape garden in Italy and the superb neo-Classic complex includes the Villa, Etruscan tomb, and many stunning features. Under the Villa and park is an extensive network of catacombs, which whilst common in Rome represent the only Jewish Catacombs here; all the others being Christian. Part of the catacombs under the Villa was turned into a bunker for the former fascist dictator of Italy, Benito Mussolini. He had them reinforced with concrete and an air-raid shelter installed, and lived in the Villa above until his death in 1943. He paid a token rent of a single lira as his annual rent.

# WIELICZKA SALT MINE
## ul.Danilowicza 10, Wieliczka, Krakow, Poland

This World Heritage Site is remarkable and is certain to astonish visitors as there is no comparable place in the world quite like it. The Wieliczka Salt Mine has been mined continuously since the Middle Ages and miners have carved elaborate underground rooms and intricate sculptures within the Miocene salt. There is a gigantic subterannean cathedral carved entirely from salt including the floor, walls and decorations, with even the glowing chandeliers being made from salt crystals.

Salt has been an economic foundation here for time immemorial. In ancient times it was used as a means of payment, and during the 14th century salt mines generated over 30% of all the State's income. Casimir the Great dictated the operating principles of the mine in 1368, and in the 16th century the Wieliczka Salt Mine became one of the largest businesses in Europe. During those days the mine had thousands of workers and even its own underground kitchens. It was also believed that salt mixed with other substances could cure a whole host of conditions including snake bites, gout, ulcers and warts. Brine baths were introduced here as a form of treatment in 1826, and it was believed that they were instrumental in treating up to 40 illnesses - even infertility and impotence. In 1958 there was a resurgence in treatment at the mine, although by the end of the 1950's this waned as steps were taken to protect the mine due to escalating tourism.

The Salt Mine in Wieliczka has always been extremely popular, from the 14th century when it was shown to the very privileged royal visitors, to today where a million visitors a year pour in to see the labyrinth of chambers, passages, and incredible structures made of salt.

*Underground cathedral.*

A place of truly cavernous proportions, the mine is on 9 levels. Excavations, chambers and lakes constitute a total length of 300 kilometres, the depth is 327 metres, and the entire complex is an illustration of the stages of development of mining technology over time. Early in the 20th century the Chapel of St.Kinga was added. Carved by miners-sculptors, its walls illustrate superb relief work decorated with scenes from the Bible. The sheer beauty is enhanced by the light of chandeliers made from crystalline salt.

*The entrance to the 3rd Infiltration Tunnel where unusual trolley-cars take you on a spooky journey through this underground borderline, and (below) a detailed plan of the Tunnel which was designed for a surprise attack on Seoul by North Korea.*

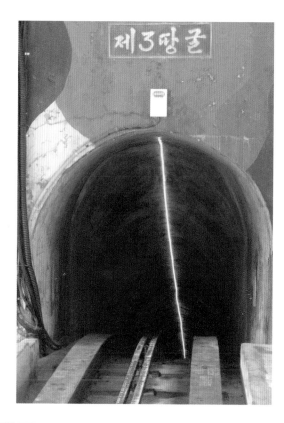

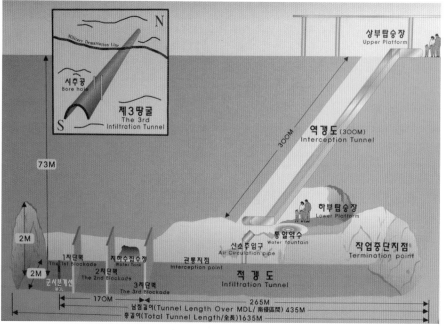

제3땅굴
The 3rd
Infiltration Tunnel

시추공
Bore hole

Military Demarcation Line

N

S

상부탑승장
Upper Platform

역갱도 (300M)
Interception Tunnel

300M

73M

하부탑승장
Lower Platform

통일약수
Water fountain

산소주입구
Air Circulation pipe

작업중단지점
Termination point

2M

2M

1차단벽
The 1st Blockade

군사분계선
MDL

2차단벽
The 2nd Blockade

3차단벽
The 3rd Blockade

지하수집수장
Water Tank

관통지점
Interception point

적갱도
Infiltration Tunnel

170M

265M

남침길이(Tunnel Length Over MDL/ 南侵區間) 435M

총길이(Total Tunnel Length/全長)1635M

# 3RD INFILTRATION TUNNEL
## DMZ, Seoul, Korea

East is east and west is west, and never the twain shall meet - so the saying goes. Well what about north and south? Particularly when we are talking about North and South Korea, a couple of countries whose previous animosity towards each other makes the 'Rambo' films look like playground tiffs.

Following the Armistice Agreement the Military Demarcation Line now divides North and South Korea, with the Demilitarized Zone (DMZ) encompassing the Armistice Line. It stretches 155 miles across the Korea Peninsula covering a huge area of 64 million sq.ft, extends 2km north and south of the Armistice Line, and it is here that armed soldiers (said to be a million) of both sides take to squaring up to each other every day with stony faces.

North Korea first began digging tunnels under the DMZ around the time of the peace talks in 1974. North Korea's President, Kim Il-sung, believed that a single tunnel would be more effective than atom bombs should the need arise to invade. There have been several major tunnels such as the 1st Infiltration Tunnel discovered in 1974 in the Western Sector of the DMZ near Gorang-po, and the 2nd and 4th Infiltration Tunnels at the Central DMZ Sector, and 26km north-east of Yanggu respectively. But it is the 3rd Infiltration Tunnel that is supposedly the most notorious and cunning, and it is now open to the public; by way of a bizarre, flat bedded tunnel-trolley, with no sides or roof, that hurtles you (strapped-in) down the steep incline entrance of a barely lit tunnel.

The 3rd Infiltration Tunnel is only 44 km from Seoul. It was planned for a massive attack on South Korea and cunningly made under the guise of being a factory. The 'factory' construction work, right at the border, synchronized explosions on the site with detonations in the tunnel, to avoid being detected. It was only the defection of a North Korean refugee that alerted South Korea to its existance. At first they did not believe him, but a series of bore holes revealed the existence of a hollow. They dug a tunnel with a 30 degrees slope to intercept the North Korean tunnel, but the North Korean workers had already gone, blackening the walls of the tunnel before fleeing. South confronted North, and North denied it existed. Then they admitted constructing it but said it was for mining coal (which is why the fleeing workers had smeared coal dust on the walls). All the dynamite holes pointed to South Korea, and there was no geologic results showing coal present in the area. No wonder there is a perpetual stand-off between these inscrutable nations.

Visitors to the DMZ can see many sights complete with many restrictions, but in the tourist-trap world we live in today there can be no more startling a sight than the 'moving floor' you are invited to step upon here. The floor of the tunnel-trolley is exactly level with the platform (which is quite disconcerting), with seats apparently glued or nailed to it. As aforementioned, there are no sides or roof, and once equipped with your hard hat and strapped in, the tunnel-trolley edges forward before whizzing down the steep descent of the tunnel. It puts most fairground rides to shame, and the surreal shadows and scenery of this underground borderline are quite spooky. Welcome to north meets south.

## ARGYLE DIAMOND MINE
### Kununurra, Kimberley, Western Australia

As the world's largest single producer of diamonds, the Argyle Diamond Mine in the Kimberley region of Western Australia offers visitors a first class look at its complex that is no different to what VIP's might expect to receive. Located in one of the world's last great wilderness regions in a remote, hot desert, where temperatures can soar to over 40 degrees, production at the mine began relatively late (1985) but approximately 30 million carats of diamonds a year are now processed from here. The diamond bearing rock is broken up by blasting and drilling before being loaded into 120-ton dump trucks. From there it is transferred to the processing plant for cleaning and gravity separation before crushing and scrubbing. The diamonds are extracted by using x-ray machines as they fluoresce under these conditions and can be easily identified.

Tours of the mine include a fly-over of the gigantic site, a guided tour of the process plant, and a visit to the recovery viewing room where rough diamonds are sorted and graded according to size and quality.

## SZTOLNIE KOWARY
### Kowary, Poland

Back in 1945 a Polish and Russian collaboration for uranium mining started at Kowary. This mine was extremely important to the Soviet Union at this time as the uranium was to produce the first Russian atomic bombs. The mining activities were very covert and top secret for decades, and substantial uranium was found bordering the granite with metamorphic rocks. Typical minerals of these deposits included silver, calcite and uraninite.

In 1963 the mine was closed, although public attention had been drawn to it when a radon therapy tunnel was opened (see also Radon Health Mine in Montana - page 56 of this book). The mined ore had been milled and leached to extract the uranium and the tailings were pumped as sludges into a sedimentation pond where, as far as we know, they still are today. This would have been a real danger to users of the radon therapy tunnel nearby although radon itself, as a natural gas, has a very low radioactivity and is not really dangerous - but also not really healthy.

In April 2000 the mine, having been converted, was opened as a tourist attraction complete with a multimedia museum. So, if you fancy glowing in the dark like a catherine wheel on bonfire night, you know where to go.

## THE CRYSTAL CAVES OF BERMUDA
### Bailey's Bay, Hamilton Parish, Bermuda

Since the island was first settled Bermuda's limestone caves have been visited, and attracted the attention of many. In 1623, Captain John Smith (of Pocahontas fame) spoke of these "dark and cumbersome caverns", but it was not until about 1906 that the magnificent Crystal Cave was to be discovered by 2 young boys attempting to retrieve a lost cricket ball which had disappeared into

*The pontoon bridge that spans the deep subterranean lake in Crystal Cave.*

a hole in the ground. The hole through which Edgar Hollis and Carl Gibbons descended to retrieve their ball is still visible today, but visitors to one of Bermuda's best tourist attractions can use a much more accessible entrance to view the boys discovery.

When the owners of the property (the Wilkinson family) were informed of the boys find they immediately set about exploring the cave. Percy Wilkinson lowered his son Bernard into the hole on 140ft of really strong rope which was tied to a tree. His 14 year old son had nothing more than a bicycle lamp to illuminate his new surroundings. What he saw was millions of years in the making; a huge crystal clear lake, said

to be 55ft deep, set in a cavern that was adorned with magnificent stalagmites and stalactites.

Your visit to The Crystal Caves of Bermuda includes not only the Crystal Cave discovered by the boys, but also its smaller sister cave, Fantasy Cave, which is a journey through geologic time. Closed to the public for decades, Fantasy Cave reopened in 2001 and is a complete contrast to the Crystal Cave.

It is not known if the 2 small boys playing cricket ever found their ball, but their loss would have been our gain as The Crystal Caves of Bermuda are a silent, still wonderland of unbelievable beauty created by Mother Nature.

# book orders & suggestions

We hope you have enjoyed reading this book and will want to purchase other titles of Strangest Books. Please see the back cover for a brief description of other titles currently available in this series.

Our books can be purchased from all good book shops and a broad selection of other retailers. Alternatively, you may wish to visit our website where excerpts and images from other titles can be viewed free of charge, and books may be ordered direct.

We are always interested in hearing from readers with any comments or suggestions. If you would like to contact us please use the relevant e-mail link below.

**e-mail direct**

bookorders@strangestbooks.co.uk

suggestions@strangestbooks.co.uk

**or visit our website at:**

http://www.strangestbooks.co.uk